MW00461800

THE LAUGHING CHERUB GUIDE TO PAST-LIFE REGRESSION:

A Handbook for Real People

by
MARY ELIZABETH RAINES

Laughing Cherub Unlimited
Weyauwega, WI
www.books-plays-scripts.com

Cover design & Illustrations by M. E. Raines
Book and cover layout by Carly Irion

Published by
Laughing Cherub Unlimited
Weyauwega, WI 54983
www.books-plays-scripts.com

ISBN 978-0-9726146-0-3

Printed in the United States of America.

This book is dedicated to all the beautiful souls who have studied past-life regression with me, and to the many who have experienced healing and transformation as a result of working with these gifted counselors.

Mary Elizabeth Raines

TABLE OF CONTENTS

"*Nothing is dead: men feign themselves dead, and endure mock funerals and mournful obituaries, and there they stand looking out of the window, sound and well, in some new and strange disguise.*"

Ralph Waldo Emerson
from the essay "Nominalist and Realist"

THE LAUGHING CHERUB GUIDE TO PAST-LIFE REGRESSION

A Handbook for Real People

by
MARY ELIZABETH RAINES

PREFACE
☙

Our past has clothed us in magnetic layers, invisible garments that have accumulated from lifetimes of experiences and choices. They mold and shape who we are today. Some of these garments are beautiful and some are ugly.

Often they are so subtle and comfortable that we are not even aware that we wear them, scarcely recognizing their soft whispers and their ever-present effects on our personality, talents, relationships, habits and deeply engrained feelings.

At other times, they gather new force and scream like a hungry demanding baby, magnetizing into our lives patterns of such urgency that we cannot move forward until we acknowledge and finally peel off the burdensome hardened layers. Our freedom comes when we find that that we need no longer carry the weight of the past as we move through life.

The purpose of this book is to acquaint people in a practical way with information about how past-life regression works and how it helps to heal. There are chapters covering the theories of reincarnation, facts about hypnosis, what happens in a past-life regression including a step-by-step walkthrough of a typical session, ways in which people heal through this process, and examples of actual past-life regressions.

The material presented has come from my own experience working in the field of past-life regression. Along the way, I have been inspired by many authors, including Kahlil Gibran, Edgar Cayce, Jess Stearn, and Joan Grant. I wish to pay particular tribute to contemporary writers Dick Sutphen and Henry Leo Bolduc, who are important pioneers and teachers in this field, and whom I am privileged to know, and I would also like to acknowledge the work of Brian Weiss.

The information that follows is not presented as absolute truth. Instead, it is offered in the hopes of helping to trigger and stimulate the thinking and beliefs of the reader.

INTRODUCTION

ભ

Why did I always know what champagne tasted like, even though I grew up in a teetotalling family?

Why, as a child, before I ever saw a movie or television, did I cower with fear whenever an airplane flew over our house?

Why did my heart soar inexplicably when my family visited Salem, Massachusetts for the first time, even though I was just a litte girl?

I first began to ponder the question of reincarnation when I was 17 years old. It was 1964. Up until that point, I had never seriously entertained the idea that we might be born more than once. As a Protestant minister's daughter, I had been trained to regard such thoughts as superstitious rubbish. According to my conventional Christian upbringing, only heathen and primitive people believed in reincarnation.

It wasn't until I was a senior in high school that I began to question my spiritual beliefs. To my dismay, when I took a hard and unflinching look at what I had always presumed to be true, there was nothing there. My spiritual landscape was empty and dry. Thus began a period in my life that was devoid of faith or belief in anything. My findings plunged me into a deep depression, and I began to spiral into that horrific inner journey which some describe as the dark night of the soul.

Throughout those difficult months, I continued to function in a reasonable way, so my family and friends never guessed how much I was suffering. I am glad that I kept my crisis private. Because of it, I was able to find answers on my own, rather than taking on the filter of someone else's beliefs. I am also grateful that that my teenaged depression occurred in the years before our present-day epidemic of treating every hint of emotional disturbance with a quick-fix prescription.

Had my adolescent spiritual pain been numbed by medication, as it is for so many today, I would never have begun the journey of discovery that, decades later, continues to transform and heal my soul.

The key to that discovery arrived in the form of a book. While in the depths of my spiritual despair, I stumbled across a copy of *The Prophet* by Kahlil Gibran. My mother had given this book to my father for Christmas that year. As such, the gift was dutifully afforded a highly visible place in our living room for several weeks before being relegated to my father's office library shelves with all the other books. One sad winter's day, out of boredom, I reached for it and began to read.

My life has never been the same. *The Prophet* proved to be the single most important book I have ever opened. Gibran's poetic and profoundly simple pages opened a doorway onto a sacred view of life that was at once vibrantly new, yet at the same time ancient and familiar. His words resonated with the deepest core of my being. The wise passages quenched my spiritual thirst. To this day, *The Prophet* remains my favorite book.

In *The Prophet*, Gibran speaks of how we are born many times to many mothers, returning again and again to this earth. A seedling from these pages was planted and took root in my belief system. Its growth was nurtured by other books, such as Paramahansa Yogananda's *Autobiography of a Yogi*, and the writings of Edgar Cayce and Joan Grant, and it was toughened by the winds of my innate skepticism and caution. Later authors like Jess

Stearn and Dick Sutphen influenced the unfolding of my understanding of reincarnation.

STILL, MY BELIEF in past lives was only a theory—until it was sealed by an experience I had when I was in my early 20s, an experience that lasted for only a few seconds. It is important for me to note that in those days, I stayed well away from the drug trips with which most of my peers were experimenting. I'd never had anything remotely resembling a hallucination or a vision, nor did I even have any successful experience with meditation. My thinking was extremely concrete.

I had moved to Boston, near the city of Salem that had so enchanted me as a child. One day I was in my Back Bay apartment, trying unsuccessfully to concentrate on reading a rather dull book. It was a chilly New England afternoon with leaden skies. Suddenly and unexpectedly something astonishing happened. A flashback zoomed into focus. I was instantly transported back to my childhood, where I clearly re-experienced lying in my bed as a very little girl of perhaps two years old, waiting to fall asleep. This little girl was remembering, as she did every night before going to sleep. And what she was remembering were all of her past lifetimes, in rich and vivid detail!

It all came back to me in a flash. I was flooded with the overwhelming familiarity of this scene, and wondered how I could ever have forgotten. Remembering my other lifetimes had been a natural aspect of my toddler world. The moments before falling asleep each night had been my special time, when I would delve into the stronghold of my ancient memories.

This astonishing flashback lasted for only a few brief, intensely vivid seconds. In that short space of time, I was completely immersed in a rich awareness of my multiple lives, each with its own color and emotion and story. It is impossible to express the depth of this flashback, the reality of it, and how amazed and stunned I was to remember *remembering*!

Almost as quickly as this portal opened for me on that Boston afternoon, it closed. I found myself being yanked unwillingly back to present awareness, and all the memories of my past lives swiftly dimmed from my mind, struggle though I might to bring them back with me. They were like a fish on the end of a line that had briefly emerged from the water, only to break free and dive back into the depths.

Those memories have never returned, but ever since that event I have been convinced that I have lived many, many lifetimes.

IN THE YEARS that followed, I launched a quest to experience an actual past-life regression. It was difficult, if not impossible. There were few people doing that kind of work in those days. Yet, I persisted, for I was determined to seek out the mysteries of my deep past. I recognized that there were serious and pressing issues in my life—inexplicable relationships, puzzling behaviors and bewildering life patterns—over which I seemed powerless. I sought answers to the core questions of my being, and became convinced that if I could only undergo a past-life regression, all of my answers would emerge in one dramatic session.

This compelling idea was enhanced when I watched a short film about past-life regression. In it, a woman suffering from chronic illness was dramatically healed after she regressed to a previous lifetime in which she found herself to be an Aztec priest who had cut out the hearts of babies in sacrificial rites. It was a highly emotional testimonial. I loved the drama, and eagerly awaited my own regression, where I would doubtlessly find some similarly spectacular past life which would explain everything about my issues and patterns in one fell swoop.

Even after I found individuals who could help me regress, however,—a search which itself took many years,—accessing my past lives was not easy for me. My journey didn't turn out to be anything like that of the woman in the film, or those in the books I'd read. It proved to be a flawed, arduous, and frustratingly slow process.

My explorations are still by no means complete. To this day, I have never discovered the single mega-lifetime that I'd hoped would provide all of my answers and solve every problem. Instead, through decades of work, I have gradually uncovered a number of past lives, with each one contributing a small piece of the puzzle.

TODAY, AS SOMEONE who has conducted many hundreds of individual and group past-life regressions and trained others in these techniques, I am grateful for the many stumbling blocks I encountered along the way. As a result of those obstacles, I learned a great deal which I am now able to share with my clients and readers-information that would not have been available to me if my process had been smooth and unhindered.

I am writing this book to offer you some of the treasures I have mined about past-life regression, facts that I wish I had known before beginning my quest. I hope that reading this will make the process easier, richer and more productive for you. In this book, you will become familiar with the step-by-step process of going through a past-life regression, including what it feels like to be hypnotized...and you will learn the magnificent ways in which we can heal our present selves by accessing our past lives.

WHAT IS REINCARNATION?

The fundamental theory of reincarnation is that our souls are reborn many times in different bodies. Earth is like a school to which we return over and over again for new experiences and the growth that results. Once we have learned a lesson, it becomes part of our soul's knowledge, and we move on to the next lesson.

If one believes that the soul is infinite, it is no more miraculous to be born many times than to be born only once—and far more reasonable.

Reincarnation is centered on the law of karma, which is the most just belief system going. It boils down to this: everything we do, positive or negative, eventually comes back to us. We reap precisely what we have sown. This is the perfect manifestation of the Golden Rule, *Do unto others as you would have others do unto you.*

Reincarnation provides us with a perfect scale of justice and fairness in a world that can otherwise appear random and cruel. It answers many of our perplexing questions, explaining why one child might be born in a comfortable home with beautiful health, while another enters life only to starve to death in a third-world country; or why one individual is always broke, but is well-loved and nurtured, while another might be wealthy, but repeatedly has harsh encounters with mean and destructive people.

We return over and over to this magnificent and oftentimes difficult school called Earth so that we may learn important lessons, reincarnating as both male and female in lives that encompass all races and cultures.

Some proponents of reincarnation believe that before entering physical form, our souls choose which lessons we need and plan opportunities for us to learn them. This may be done with assistance from guides. Others feel that our lessons are assigned to us by a higher power or other entities outside of ourselves. In either instance, we are meant to grow and improve.

Many, if not all, of our life circumstances may be foreordained for the purpose of this positive forward movement. While we may not be able to alter the circumstances themselves, we can always change the way in which we respond to them. Our thoughts and feelings are our own to do with as we wish. There is always opportunity for growth through our choices and attitudes. These choices usually involve our responses to what life hands us.

We may have circumstances of wealth, for instance, in which we are offered the choice between haughty aloofness or compassionate generosity; or we may experience oppression, and have the option either of stewing in resentment or choosing instead to forgive. Themes like love, patience, kindness, responsibility, selflessness, integrity, courage and forgiveness turn up over and over again in the regressions I do with people.

A girl is in a car accident that causes her to become a paraplegic for the rest of her life, confined to a wheelchair. This occurs as a karmic debt from a previous lifetime when she was a Korean soldier who planted a land mine that crippled a child.

Not only is she paying a karmic debt; her inability to walk will also offer her the opportunities she most needs for the specific growth her soul requires. Through the limitations of her circumstances, her most important—and difficult!—life choice will be whether to hold onto bitterness and resentment for the rest of her days, or to become more loving, accepting and compassionate.

LIFE SCHOOL IS not easy, and we do not always make the choices that permit us to accelerate our growth. If we fail to make the correct choice in one lifetime, however, it is certain that we will continue to have ample opportunities to do so! Each incarnation we have experienced has something important to contribute to the whole of the soul. A person's status, IQ, wealth or popularity in a particular lifetime in no way indicates how evolved her or his soul might be. Success as we measure it in our society today is very different from the success our souls desire, which has nothing whatsoever to do with social status, intelligence, money or how well liked we are. We have all arrived at this destination with different assignments and different lessons to learn.

One woman's lessons in this lifetime may involve becoming a superstar in order to learn how to handle fame and its attendant power. Another might live on a street corner as an alcoholic derelict and bag lady so that she can be taught those lessons that come with the experience of extreme humility, addiction and degradation. Similarly, someone who is the victim of persecution may have had a karmic debt to pay, while that person's oppressor may have taken on such a role to enable her or him to understand both brutality and compassion more thoroughly, and to afford the oppressor the choice of ending a cycle of violence. We all take turns being rich and poor, smart and stupid, the good guy and the bad guy.

The limitations of our lives in human form offer us a splendid opportunity to grow and expand. We seem to learn better from pressures and difficulties. If we are unable to learn the lesson thoroughly in one lifetime, we will return until we get it right. Although earth school is tough, it is generous. There are no straight-A students and there is no honor roll; yet every one of its students is ultimately guaranteed to succeed!

Just because our souls are eternal and elastic does not mean that we should accept injustice or deaden our compassion. A belief in reincarnation is not an excuse to harden our hearts against suffering—to shrug off terrible events that happen to others, blaming it on their bad karma. Indeed, those experiencing lifetimes of suffering may be doing so to balance a previous misdeed, or because they have chosen to learn how to become more compassionate in the fastest and most efficient way possible.

Whatever we observe happening to others has undoubtedly happened to us as well. Realizing that we have all been born multiple times in multiple circumstances permits us to recognize that all souls are truly equal and that we are indeed one.

In my experience of conducting many past-life regressions, the major issues which people confront and subsequently learn from their previous lifetimes are those of opening their hearts, learning to love, dealing honorably with adversity, and remaining true to important principles.

HOW OFTEN DO WE REINCARNATE?

CR

There are multitudes of theories about the finer points of reincarnation. Some of these theories are very elaborate, with an abundance of levels, rules and structures that may be tied into specific religious beliefs. Others are quite simple. I urge you to remain both open-minded and cautious in this interesting exploration.

Some schools of thought claim to know the precise number of lifetimes each individual must go through, and exactly how much time elapses between lives. People have told me about receiving very emphatic statements from psychics or religious leaders about how many lifetimes they have had and how many more are going to be required, such as, *"Each of us has seventy-three lifetimes which are all precisely 200 years apart, and you are presently in your 15th incarnation."*

I would urge caution when hearing such a statement. Psychics or religious leaders may indeed be able to travel to realms where the veil is thinner and truth is more evident to them than to the average individual, but they are still people with their own filters of perception and their own agendas. There is no single person who is privy to the complete truth.

In present-day Western culture most people tend towards the belief that our souls return as often as necessary, and that the length of time between lives is very elastic. According to this thought, some souls, such as those who die prematurely or who have unfinished business, may be reborn immediately, while others experience a lengthier wait between lives, depending upon their urgency to return and what they are slated to learn.

I know people who have been told by psychics that they are on their last lifetime, or who firmly believe that they themselves can stop the cycle of human lifetimes whenever they want and claim, *"This is my final lifetime. I don't want to come back any longer."*

Perhaps this is so, but it is more likely to be wishful thinking. If we don't want to come back because life or other people are intolerable to us or because of any kind of disgust or dismay with human existence, it is almost certain that we will come back so that we may learn how to form brighter, more all-encompassing attitudes! Although no one knows for certain, in agreeing to experience human form, we have apparently entered into a very binding kind of contract, and we will not be finished with our cycle of lives on this planet until we have completed the contract and learned all the lessons that a soul can learn.

PARENTS AND CHILDREN

CR

Most contemporary proponents of reincarnation state that we choose our parents before being born. This does not mean that whenever there is a wise and loving couple on earth, there are hordes of souls lined up in the hope of selecting them as parents! Since struggle and obstacles offer much more fertile ground for growth than ease and comfort do, the parents we select are those who can provide the best framework for our growth and bring us to the circumstances most necessary to complete our soul's mission, whether those circumstances are interpreted as positive or negative.

Understanding that we choose our parents makes us pause when we are ready to shift the blame for our troubles onto them or our backgrounds, and gives us the opportunity to take more responsibility for ourselves.

> *Guillermo* was born into a poor Hispanic family in the Southwest to alcoholic parents who abused him. He grew up in a crime-ridden neighborhood full of gang violence. In his struggle to overcome this background, he fought to get a good education and eventually became financially successful. He is now on his way to becoming an inspirational leader and motivational speaker.*
>
> *He believes that his soul purposefully chose to incarnate in difficult circumstances to parents of limited*

ability. Because of these conditions, he is a man of far broader compassion and wisdom than he would have possessed had he been born into an indulgent and wealthy family on the right side of the tracks.

(*The names and certain non-essential information of all individuals mentioned in this book have been changed to protect their anonymity.)*

SOME SAY THAT certain less-evolved souls are opportunists, frantic to re-enter the earth cycle quickly. These souls rashly plunge into a physical body wherever there is an opening (a pregnancy!) without first considering the parents or the life lessons involved.

Just as in every other aspect of reincarnation, there is debate about the moment the soul enters the human form. There are those who argue that this does not occur until just before or even slightly after birth; others say that the soul enters at the exact moment of conception; while still others believe that during pregnancy, the soul lives primarily in the world of spirit while being only occasionally present in the fetus. A soul may actually enter into a pregnancy with the foreknowledge that it will be terminated by a miscarriage or an abortion so that it may have that experience...or offer that experience to the mother.

This leads to a fascinating theory, which is that certain highly evolved souls come into form only briefly, or enter badly debilitated bodies, for the sole purpose of serving others who need to learn their life's lessons. It is thought to be one of the most enlightened and loving forms of selfless service. According to this school of thought, a baby who dies shortly after birth or a severely retarded person may actually be an extremely advanced soul.

LAUGHTER AND TEARS

CR

Although we grow stronger through difficult experiences and challenges, life in form on this planet is also meant to be appreciated and enjoyed. The law of karma is that of perfect balance. This extends to the perfect balance between tears and laughter. Most past lives, even those that appear to be harsh, are combinations of sorrow and joy.

Some claim that after a cycle of difficult learning experiences, we are granted—or offer ourselves—an easy and restful lifetime, almost like a vacation. Even when enduring the hardest lifetimes, however, our days are not wholly sad. There can be moments of enormous beauty, laughter and happiness in the most difficult life.

After a typical past-life regression, I take people through a life review, where they meet with guides or teachers and receive knowledge and higher awareness of the lifetime they just experienced. In these life reviews, people often realize that a vitally important aspect of their lessons has been to expand their appreciation of the benefits of being in form, such as loving their partners or family, enjoying the beauty of nature, or rejoicing in an ability.

Indeed, when we come to the realization that our circumstances are always changing, that we are responsible for everything that occurs to us, and that we will inevitably grow from it, we can discover a certain sweetness even in our tears.

FRIENDS, GROUPS AND SOULMATES

ও

Have you ever felt an immediate and strong connection to a person or a group, right after meeting them? Have you been in a workplace or class where everyone bonded closely and your relationships and experiences, whether positive or negative, seemed more intense than usual? Most proponents of reincarnation state that in such situations, we are meeting people we have known in previous lifetimes.

Many believe that we reincarnate over and over with people we have known before-that we are brought together repeatedly with the same soul group, because we have group lessons to learn as well as our individual lessons. Included in this is the belief that each nation has its own karma.

Soul mates are thought to be those with whom we have shared numerous past lives and deep bonds of love. Some believe that a soul mate is the perfect partner, usually someone with whom we have sexual as well as romantic ties. Others believe that a soul mate may arrive in a more platonic package, like a relative or dear friend for whom we feel great love or with whom we do important work.

It has even been suggested that soul mates offer loving service by entering our lives to teach us our most crucial lessons, which may not necessarily be pleasant ones. Thus, the worst enemy we encounter may actually be our soul mate, who has undertaken this role so that we may learn difficult lessons.

According to different theories, we also have twin

souls—entities who literally share the same soul with us. Like soul mates, these twin souls may appear as our partners, family members or good friends.

The nature of our relationships with a loved one changes from lifetime to lifetime. An individual who was someone's father in a previous incarnation may be that person's sister or best friend in another; a favorite teacher from times past may be reborn as a nephew. Not every close relationship in our lives is someone we knew from the past, however, and we do not always come back with the same people. It depends upon the experiences we are slated to have. When our paths cross briefly with someone with whom we feel a deep connection, that individual may have had an important relationship with us in a past life but may not have any important part to play in our current lifetime.

RUTH, AN ISRAELI woman, regressed to a past life in which she was a Jewish woman named Ida who had teenaged daughter named Sophie. The lifetime she experienced took place during the Holocaust of World War II. Mother and daughter were both taken to a concentration camp, where Ida was shot and killed.

In Ruth's present life, she was born a few years after the end of World War II. She arrived as the daughter of Sophie, the same woman who had earlier been her daughter. Sophie had survived the death camp. Ruth discovered that she had been her own grandmother!

The realization made sense to her, and explained the mysterious compulsion she possessed, even as a young girl, to act in a protective and parental way towards her mother.

THEORIES AND CHALLENGES

❧

There are those who believe that we are all one, all emerging from the same source. We fragment into individual personalities to have experiences in human form, and then return to the whole after the death of the body. According to this belief, we can access all the memories of anyone who has ever lived. They are us; you are me. When we are being regressed to a past life, our soul simply selects a memory from the pool which is pertinent to our current issues.

A variation on this theory is that we have an infinite number of lives in which we ultimately experience everything there is to experience. We have related in various ways—sometimes positively, sometimes negatively—with every other individual and will continue to do so.

Some traditions teach that souls migrate between species. In my practice, I have rarely encountered this. A close friend, however, once revealed having had a vivid recollection of being a giant sea turtle who was caught by Japanese fisherman in very ancient days. Another individual, who was regressed by one of my students, had the past-life memory of being a gorilla.

There are those who scoff at reincarnation by stating that the population of the world is currently so huge that it would be impossible for all of us to have had past lives. Previous human populations in our planet's history were so much smaller that, even when all their numbers are added together, they do not total the billions of people now inhabiting the earth, thus making it technically impossible for all of us to have lived even one past life, much less dozens of them.

That objection is overruled by the interesting speculation that our souls may be experiencing any number of lives at once, and that we live multiple lifetimes simultaneously. These lifetimes may be parallel or overlapping. According to this theory, someone who was born in Chicago in 1967 may also have had a life as an Egyptian street vendor who died in 1973. Taking that a step further is the belief that there is no such thing as time, and all of our lives, even those purportedly in the past, are occurring simultaneously.

THEORIES AND BELIEFS about past lives abound. I do not pretend to know what the real truth is, and suggest that you consider remaining open as well. Not knowing offers us a curious freedom. Remember that you are as privy to the truth as any other human being.

Dorothy Ackerman, a Quaker friend and one of my important mentors in reincarnation techniques, once said to me, *"We are all in boarding school. Earth is the school, and our bodies are our uniforms. When we die, all it means is that we get to take off our uniform and go home."*

IS REINCARNATION REAL OR A FANTASY?

CR

Recently a young man said to me, *"I don't believe in reincarnation...and I didn't in my last life, either!"*

Bookstore and library shelves contain books written about people who have had uncanny remembrances of former lifetimes. Some include very specific details that have been validated. Certainly the majority of people who come to me for past-life regression have experiences that appear to be authentic. Oftentimes this sense of authenticity stems from the individual having a strong emotional involvement with the lifetime being recalled.

> *Frank came for a past-life regression, but expressed grave doubts about his ability to do so. He was very resistant to the process. Despite using all the resources I could summon, he had a difficult time accessing a past life. After Frank concluded that he probably couldn't regress, he was able to relax...and suddenly began reliving a former lifetime as a simple Amish farmer. When the vivid images of his farmhouse and beloved wife came into his mind, he began to weep tears of recognition and joy.*

Sometimes people who are regressed to former lifetimes experience sensations, like a bad odor or a horrible taste, which are so overwhelming that they leave no doubt about the validity of what they are remembering.

Lisa re-lived a previous lifetime in which she had been a man who died from a gunshot wound. She kept wrinkling her face in disgust, because she had such an acute memory of the sharp, unpleasant taste of blood in her mouth.

Other validations occur when individuals have automatic, unthinking responses during their regressions that make perfect historical sense-responses that they would not have had the time to fabricate.

Annette, who wanted to understand why she was a compulsive overeater, regressed to a lifetime as a Roman soldier. She found herself in a strange foreign city, and described the way the streets and buildings looked. When asked the location of the city, she replied, "I don't know where I am. They never tell us where we're going."

The logic of her answer was convincing, for it is doubtlessly correct that nobody held up maps or explained to the ancient Roman foot-soldiers precisely where they were headed on their marches.

In that same memory, the Roman soldier broke the rules by leaving camp and pillaging in abandoned houses in the town that had just been conquered. In her narrative, Annette remarked that he never discovered anything of value when he did that; to expect to find valuables in such humble dwellings would be absurd. Nor was he interested in intimidating or attacking the few huddled women who had not managed to escape before the army arrived. What he really hoped to find was extra food, for the soldiers were not fed adequately and he was always hungry. The best "loot" he ever rooted up was a round loaf of bread in a basket.

After the session, it was pointed out by an observer that Roman historians boasted of how well fed their armies were. According to the woman who had been regressed—at least at the point in time she was remembering—this was simply propaganda and the truth was quite different.

Brad had the grisly recollection of being a woman who was disemboweled and then, while barely still living, having her arms and legs chained to four horses, who were going to pull her apart. He remembered the tremendous physical agony she was in, and how long it seemed to take to chain her to the horses. Almost as soon as the horses began pulling, however, he sighed with relief. The pain suddenly disappeared! For a few brief seconds before the woman died, her body was free of suffering.

After emerging from his session, Brad deduced with some astonishment that the violent pull of the horses must have made something in the woman's spine snap, and this had left her in the final seconds of life free from all physical sensation, foiling the intent of her persecutors.

Ani, a French woman, was regressed and found herself living with a small tribe in a place which had a warm climate. Ani described herself as having dark skin in her past life. Her dwelling was a simple hut with an earthen floor, and her usual meals consisted of some sort of cooked grain. When I suggested that she speak her name, it came from her throat as a guttural, odd sound.

She was forced to marry a man she did not love, and had a son with him. She felt alienated from her husband and her child, and avoided being with them as much as possible.

Ani's next remembrance during the regression was of being on a sailing ship on a large body of water. The boat was crowded; there were many others with her. She was excited and full of eager anticipation. Asked how she had gotten on the ship, she related that she and the others had been presented with an opportunity to sail to a distant place where they could create a new and better life. Her husband and son had not wanted to go, and she had gladly left them behind.

As she was re-experiencing this incident, her smiles suddenly turned to tears and her face filled with fear. Asked what was happening, she replied, "I'm naked. I'm scared." Upon arrival on the new shore, events had taken a suddenly harsh turn. It turned out that she and the others on the ship had been lured with false promises to keep them calm during the voyage. In fact, they ended up being sold into slavery.

The information Brad's and Ani's stories present is not something that would readily be invented, and both stories strike an authentic note.

Opponents of reincarnation point out that because of our

present-day exposure to multitudes of films and books, our sub-conscious minds have more than ample material to fabricate multiple lives, which we absorb and then "remember" as our own. Self-delusion is certainly possible. An individual may have a deep-seated need to believe that they were in a position of power in a past life, for instance, when that may not have been the case. Occasionally I have regressed people whose experiences were obviously, albeit unconsciously, contrived, with scenes they may have unwittingly pulled from movies or books. Such memories usually have a different tone to them, and include highly improbable elements or blatant historical inaccuracies.

Whether reincarnation is actual fact or fantasy, however, doesn't really matter. What does matter is that people find the answers and release/relief they are seeking. Any information that helps an individual's self-understanding is valuable, whether its source is from a former existence in another body, or whether it arises from a person's present-day subconscious.

As long as people receive the healing and release that they desire, it makes no difference whether or not what they remember is the truth.

The goal of a past-life regression is not to prove or disprove anything. The goal is to experience healing, self-knowledge and growth!

WHY WOULD I WANT TO BE REGRESSED TO A PAST LIFE?

 object

Past-life regression offers us profound insights and revelations about the journey of our soul.

- *We receive guidance, answers and assurance.*

- *We become aware of our innate gifts and abilities.*

- *We crack open the shell of limitation that surrounds us, and our lives become fuller and enriched as a result.*

- *We discover the source of our deeply engrained patterns.*

- *We recognize vastly expanded connections to people and places.*

- *We learn to take responsibility for ourselves.*

- *We have the opportunity to heal on many levels.*

The most wonderful benefit of past-life regression is when it helps us to find clues from the past that explain our puzzling behaviors and symptoms, and, through our remembrance, allows us to release the stuck pattern, forgive, heal and move forward.

WHAT IS KARMA?

ೞ

*Everything we have ever thought, felt, said or done
comes back to us in exact measure.*

The above statement is the bottom line of karma. It is exquisite, perfect justice. It allows for no blame, no excuses, no victims. The law of karma says that whatever occurs in our lives is the result of our own past choices and actions. We are responsible for every thought, emotion, word and deed that goes forth from us, and hence we are responsible for every thought, emotion, word and deed that comes back to us.

Here is a simple example of the miraculous way in which the perfect law of karma works: If we were to take something—even as small as a paper clip—which does not belong to us, something that does belong to us will in turn eventually be taken away. Conversely, if something—even as small as a paper clip—is stolen from us, at some point in time we will receive its equivalent!

An individual who was a malicious gossip in a previous lifetime might find that she suffers because others now talk about her behind her back. A person who becomes the victim of a random wild-animal attack might discover that in a past life he once abused nature by killing animals for sport. Another who is burdened with harsh responsibilities might be compensating for a lifetime of irresponsibility.

*Diane was suffering because she'd had a lover who
had ultimately hurt and rejected her in what she de-*

scribed as a very cold-hearted, cruel fashion. Exploring her past lives, Diane went back to a lifetime in ancient India. She saw herself as a woman whose frail husband was nearing death.

There was a special building where bodies of the deceased were brought and prepared in alcoves on stone slabs. The woman heartlessly brought her dying husband to this place while he was yet alive, because it was less of a nuisance to her. She sat by him as he lay on the stone, and she waited impatiently for him to die. Although his frightened eyes pleaded with her, she offered no comfort or compassion, but only looked upon him with cold disgust for the inconvenience he was causing her.

After Diane's regression, the rejection she had suffered from her former lover made sense to her, and she no longer had a need to wallow in feelings of victimization.

WHAT IS MOST important to remember about the law of karma is that we continually have choices before us. Each of our choices has a price tag attached to it. When a selfish, greedy or fearful choice is made, payment can be deferred for a long time, but the price to be paid is inevitable, and it can be very high indeed!

How long does it take before our actions, positive or negative, boomerang back to us? It appears to be anywhere from a very brief wait to many long centuries. Think of a kind of cosmic trust account holding onto the funds, waiting for the lifetime when we have particular lessons to learn before the account can be opened. Some believe that very advanced souls receive their karmic payback almost immediately, sometimes within hours or days.

In the intensity of past-life explorations, our focus is often drawn only to the grim side of the karmic balance scales because that is what is crying out for healing. We sometimes forget that we all have perpetrated many, many acts of goodness and kindness. We have all done good things, and undoubtedly made numerous choices that were loving and selfless. We've also had plenty of fun in our past lives!

When Diane regressed to being the wife in ancient India who was so cruel to her dying husband, she also remembered another event—a joyous time of celebration and festivities, where she saw splendidly decorated elephants and gaily danced with colorful crowds on the streets.

ON OCCASION, WHEN a person realizes how precisely accountable we really are for everything that occurs in our lives, a curious kind of heartlessness may set in. After a catastrophe, for example, I have heard some people shrug off the cruel events by stating that those who were hurt or killed were karmically responsible for attracting that kind of situation into their lives.

Pain is pain, however, regardless of its source. Being judgmental or callous to another's suffering is yet another choice, and probably an exceedingly unwise one, as it may well create a very ugly kind of karma in and of itself. When someone is hurting, as fellow and interconnected human beings, it behooves us to be compassionate and loving, regardless of how or why that suffering came upon the individual. Learning the laws of karma gives us the opportunity to deepen our service to humanity, as well as to begin to take responsibility for our own actions and lives.

The lessons we learn as a result of this amazing system of justice called karma cannot be categorized. They are complex, and unique to each individual. Eventually such lessons teach us, through direct experience, how to behave while inhabiting human form. Along the way we accumulate positive qualities like compassion, mercy, humor, patience, courage, fairness, trust and love.

MANIFESTATION

ও

Some proponents of past-life regression believe that the karmic events in our lives have been planned and scheduled by a power greater than ourselves, be it God, our own Higher Self, the Lords of Karma, a panel of Guides, or some other force.

An increasingly popular belief in today's culture, however, is that we alone are responsible for orchestrating our lives and the events that occur to us. Much has been written recently about our power to create and manifest, suggesting that everything that occurs to us—our economic state, our relationships, our health, and every other aspect of our lives—comes about as the result of our emotions and thought projections.

People who subscribe to such theories of manifestation some- times experience bewilderment, frustration and self-blame when they bump up against a tough circumstance such as economic hardship or illness. They wonder what they have done wrong.

While the laws of karma suggest that it is ultimately and per- fectly true that we have the ability to manifest with precision what- ever comes into our lives, this belief needs to be seasoned with the understanding that it can take generations, rather than days or weeks, for what we have created to bounce back to us. While very enlightened souls might indeed reap the consequences of their thoughts, emotions and actions almost immediately, most of us do not fit into this category. What manifests in our lives may be the result of events that were put into place centuries ago.

Regardless of whether we believe that we alone manifest our

own circumstances or whether we subscribe to the belief there is an outside agency that organizes our karma, it is crucial for us to recognize that our soul's purpose on this earth is not solely to have the easiest and smoothest ride possible. If we go to a carnival only to ride the kiddy carts, because they're safe and close to the ground, we're missing a lot. How much more expanded we become when we ride the Ferris wheel and the roller coaster!

Our souls have not come into form on earth to play it safe, but to grow, learn and stretch so that we may ultimately embrace everything that we encounter with love and light.

WILL I FIND OUT THAT I WAS SOMEONE FAMOUS, LIKE CLEOPATRA OR NAPOLEON?

൪

Probably not. It is very, very rare that anyone recalls being famous. Critics of past-life regression are fond of pointing out that everyone always remembers being Cleopatra or Napoleon. In fact, this is not true.

I have never regressed anyone who recalled being a well-known historical figure. Notable past-life regressionist and author Henry Leo Bolduc, who has conducted thousands of past-life regressions, similarly states that while he has worked with people who brought forth memories of having associations with famous people of the past, such as being a member of a royal court, in over 40 years he never once hypnotized anyone who was herself or himself a famous historical personality.

The majority of people who experience past-life regression remember lives of simplicity and even of relative humility. More often than not, those I've regressed have gone back to lifetimes where they were simple farmers, sailors, maids, servants, house-holders, tribal members and peasants. Sometimes people who are attached to melodrama arrive for their sessions with expectations of high drama or glamour, and feel let down when they remember being, say, a potato farmer with arthritis!

In a standard past-life regression, I offer people the opportunity to review the three most important events that occurred during their previous life. Apart from one or two key moments in which something unusual occurred or a vital choice was made, the notable aspects of their past lives are generally quite ordinary. In fact, when reviewing important lifetime events, over and over again people whom I regress go to two events: the birth of a child, and a wedding (or whatever served as a marriage ceremony in their culture). The wedding is either their own or that of a child. Even today, such ceremonies are indeed a major highlight in the lives of most people, and would be so even more for someone living in simpler times. The birth of a child similarly is an important and impacting event, often accompanied by great emotion and excitement.

The fact is, most of us did not have glamorous or even extraordinarily eventful past lives, at least by TV movie-of-the-week standards. To me, this is an excellent indicator of the validity of reincarnation. If all past-life memories were merely fantasies, people would doubtlessly invent situations much more colorful and exciting than the majority of stories I hear! Yet, each past life contains a valuable portion of our soul lessons and accumulated knowledge, without which we would be incomplete. Each lifetime contributes an important note in the extraordinary symphony of our lives.

JEAN CAME TO me with issues that revolved around a man to whom she was attracted. She felt extraordinarily shy and inferior whenever she was in his presence, even though socially and educationally he was not up to her level.

Before her regression, Jean admitted having an inkling that she may have had a past life as a slave on a plantation in the deep south. She'd always identified keenly with stories of black slaves. As she wondered about what may have happened in her past, she imagined that perhaps she had been a male slave who had fallen in love with the mistress of the plantation and had subsequently been lynched. Jean speculated that the mistress may have reincarnated as the man who currently made her so uncomfortable.

When she went into regression, Jean vividly recalled being a black slave, a male, but his life was far less melodramatic than the one she had imagined. The man who aroused such a sense of intimidation in Jean in her current lifetime turned out to be the owner of the plantation, which explained the nervous deference she felt when she was around him. The slave took care of his owner's horses and drove the carriage. He never married. He liked music. His years were very uneventful. He was treated decently, and died peacefully at an old age.

A story such as Jean's would never be aired on TV shows about reincarnation, which use only the most melodramatic tales and condense them into brief sound bites. It probably wouldn't make the pages of a best seller on past lives either. Nevertheless, it was exactly appropriate for what she needed to know.

It is not the drama of a past life that makes it fruitful and compelling. It is the choices and determinations that we made in our past that are important, for it is these that have created our patterns.

WHAT METHODS ARE USED TO RECALL PAST LIVES?

ဢ

Hypnosis is the most traditional and dependable method used for past-life regression. There will be more about hypnosis later in this book. Past lives may be accessed by other means as well.

One of my students once looked absently into the mirror when he was shaving, and was shocked to see another face looking back at him—his face from a previous lifetime. (See Todd's story at the end of this book.) It is not uncommon for the people with whom I've done regression work to report having had what they often describe as a "flash," where a little bit of a past life occasionally springs into their consciousness, almost like a teaser. Others have repetitive dreams which appear to link to a past life.

People's memories are sometimes triggered when they are reading. Meditation, daydreams, or hypnagogic states (the state between waking and sleeping) can bring about the emergence of a past-life recollection. Certain very intuitive individuals are fortunate enough to carry clear and conscious memories of their former incarnations.

People sometimes tune in to past lives during energy or bodywork, such as massage or Reiki. When this occurs, it is because they have actually gone into a hypnotic state during their session. If the practitioner working with them has been trained appropriately in past-life guidance, the regression can be as fruitful as a past-life session with a hypnotist.

Several of my own former lifetimes have been revealed very vividly in dreams.

The most profound of these memories emerged when I dreamt that I was on a brutal Nazi death march in Czechoslovakia at the end of World War II. I was a woman. Along with others, I was forced to march down pleasant, narrow lanes. It was early spring. There were tall, beautiful hedges that arched in over the road, and the air was fragrant and fresh. The setting should have been idyllic. Instead, it was the most excruciating experience I have ever known, both physically and mentally. I was in complete agony; it is impossible to describe the intensity of that suffering.

Upon awakening, I dismissed the dream because I mistakenly thought that there had been no such marches through Czechoslovakia. The experience, however, was so hauntingly vivid and painful—and so very removed from the feelings and thoughts I have in my present life—that I began to research the subject of the Holocaust almost obsessively. Years after the dream, to my surprise I learned that indeed there had been death marches through Czechoslovakia, and that the lanes I had seen were characteristic of the countryside in certain places where Nazi victims had been marched. I now believe that my dream was an accurate glimpse of a very unfortunate moment in a past life.

PSYCHICS ARE SOMETIMES able to see the past lives of another person. Edgar Cayce, the famous seer known as the Sleeping Prophet, achieved fame by giving thousands of life readings for people in the 1900s at a time when past-life regression was largely scorned by Western society. While in trance, this conservative Sunday School teacher discovered—at first, to his dismay!—that he was able to receive clear information about people's past lives. His readings were helpful and healing.

A psychic reading is different from a past-life regression, however. Although this method of looking at one's history can be useful, it comes, nevertheless, through the filter of someone else's perception. Most psychics will readily admit that they do not always have 100-percent accuracy when they give readings.

Two very well-known and respected psychics have written on separate occasions about individuals whom they claim had past lives in which they were burned at the stake as witches in Salem, Massachusetts, a town whose history I have explored because of my own favorable lifetimes there. The truth is that nobody in the United States has ever been burned as a witch. These psychics undoubtedly picked up something tragic and interpreted the events they saw through the lens of their incomplete understanding, distorting what actually may have happened. Even Edgar Cayce was not infallible as far as historical accuracy in the past-life readings he gave.

Even if the past life that has been viewed by someone else is totally authentic, it would be impossible for an intuitive person to convey all of the emotions and details involved. A psychic reading does not offer the opportunities for understanding and healing that one can receive by experiencing a past-life regression directly.

The very best and simplest way for most of us to access our former lifetimes is to be hypnotized by someone who is expert in past-life regression. This usually entails relaxing both our physical bodies and our thoughts, leaving us free to explore our memories. Besides the obvious benefit of having the hypnotist act as a guide during the regression, we also have someone there to witness our journey when we are hypnotized. Something in our human nature seeks to have another person present as a witness for the most profound healing to occur.

ELEVEN QUESTIONS AND ANSWERS ABOUT HYPNOSIS

ೞ

1. WHAT IF I CAN'T BE HYPNOTIZED?

THIS IS PROBABLY the number one question I am asked when people are inquiring for the first time about past-life regression. The good news is that nearly everyone can be hypnotized! It is a natural state that is easy to achieve.

All hypnosis is actually self-hypnosis. The hypnotist is simply an expert guide who can help you get there easily and efficiently. You do the driving; the hypnotist has the map and knows the shortcuts. It's simple. All you need to do is to follow the hypnotist's directions.

Only a very small percentage of the human population cannot by hypnotized, including some psychotics, people on medications or drugs that alter brain function, babies and very young children, and those with extremely low IQs. Included on this list is anyone who actively chooses to resist being hypnotized. Nearly everyone else can be hypnotized to some degree.

All that is required to enter hypnosis is average intelligence and a normal ability to hold a train of thought. Although some studies show that entering a hypnotic state is easier for people who are bright and who have good imaginations, the key factor is your willingness to cooperate with the instructions of the person guiding you (the hypnotist).

2. WILL THE HYPNOTIST CONTROL MY MIND?

NO, NOT AT all! No matter how deeply hypnotized you are, no one else can gain power over your mind. Imagine how many unscrupulous people would become hypnotists if that were possible, and how rich they'd be! You will never lose control in hypnosis, you will not unwillingly reveal secrets, nor will you do anything you don't chose to do. Thus, you may safely relax and enjoy the experience.

Sometimes when I share this information with people, they bring up stage hypnosis shows they've seen where the volunteers on stage are made to do ridiculous and seemingly embarrassing things. Understand that if these volunteers are asked to do anything that truly goes against their moral grain, they will refuse, no matter how deeply hypnotized they were. I have been a stage hypnotist, and I know this is true! The volunteers are on stage because some part of them truly enjoys performing and doing stunts that entertain the rest of us, and they have agreed to cooperate with the hypnotist for that end.

3. WHAT IS HYPNOSIS, ANYHOW?

HYPNOSIS IS A state of mind where the conscious, wakeful mind of an individual relaxes its guard—you might say that it takes a little "coffee break"—leaving the subconscious mind open to suggestions for change or improvement. Memories become more accessible, intuitive faculties are heightened, and one can become more aware of higher guidance.

Some states of hypnosis, such as that which we enter for past-life regression, have measurable brain wave frequencies different from both sleep and alert consciousness. There can be physiological changes as well. The pupils of a deeply hypnotized person whose eyes are open will not contract when a light is shined into them.

4. DOES BEING HYPNOTIZED FEEL WEIRD?

NO. MOST PEOPLE experience hypnosis as a pleasant and normal sensation of deep relaxation. In fact, all of us go in and out of light hypnotic states every day. An example of this is daydreaming. Hypnosis is such a natural state that a person emerging from a session sometimes questions whether he or she has actually been hypnotized.

5. WILL I FORGET EVERYTHING THAT HAPPENS DURING MY SESSION?

THIS IS A fear that many people bring up about hypnosis. The majority of people remain fully aware of all that occurs during their sessions and remember perfectly. Forgetting is infrequent, and usually only happens with a small percentage of the population called somnambulists. Certain somnambulists tend to have spontaneous amnesia after their sessions, although their memories will often return to them gradually. If this is a concern for you, ask your hypnotist to suggest to you that you will remember everything that has happened, and you will. I always make sure that people I'm regressing to a past life receive the suggestion that they will remember their session fully.

6. AM I GOING TO LOSE CONTROL WHEN I'M HYPNOTIZED?

NO. THE PERSON being hypnotized is always in control. You can emerge from hypnosis any time you desire. No matter how deeply hypnotized you are, you can always respond appropriately to any emergency. You can't be hypnotized to do anything you don't want to do, so you won't reveal any personal secrets or accept any suggestions that go against your ethical and moral codes.

7. WON'T BEING HYPNOTIZED WEAKEN MY WILL?

ON THE CONTRARY, hypnosis is frequently used to strengthen a person's will, such as boosting someone's ability to stop smoking.

8. WHAT IF MY HYPNOTIST HAS A HEART ATTACK DURING A SESSION? WILL I BE STUCK IN HYPNOSIS?

NO. YOU CANNOT be stuck in hypnosis. You would either fall asleep or wake up...and, I hope, perform CPR!

9. IS IT TRUE THAT EACH TIME I AM HYPNOTIZED, IT BECOMES EASIER FOR ME TO ENTER A HYPNOTIC STATE?

YES. HYPNOSIS IS like a muscle. The more it is exercised, the better it performs.

10. WILL THE HYPNOTIST MAKE ME RUN AROUND THE ROOM AND IMITATE ELVIS?

NOT UNLESS YOU discover that you are the reincarnation of Elvis! (See notes under *"Will I find out I was someone famous, like Cleopatra or Napoleon?"*)

11. WHAT DOES IT FEEL LIKE TO BE HYPNOTIZED?

IT IS NOT uncommon for people who have never been hypnotized before to imagine that they will enter some kind of zombie-like state in hypnosis. I used to imagine that myself! It doesn't happen that way, though. Hypnosis is actually an everyday, natural state. Sometimes hypnosis is described as a state similar to being in a deep daydream. Others say that it feels like incredible relaxation combined with very focused attention.

Have you ever been driving, gotten lost in thought and suddenly arrived at your destination without remembering the details of the drive there? That common effect is a form of hypnosis called road hypnosis. Being completely absorbed in a movie or a game on television is another example of a hypnotic state. It's a very normal sensation where, rather than being diffuse, the attention is actually zeroed in quite specifically on one thing.

Hypnosis is neither wakefulness nor sleep, but rests on that ledge between them. Thus, we all experience hypnosis at least twice a day: when we first wake up, and just before we drift into sleep.

Another word for the state of being in hypnosis is trance. About one in every ten or 15 people who are hypnotized can reach the deepest trance levels very readily. Such people are called somnambulists, derived from a word meaning sleepwalkers. They have an innate ability to be hypnotized easily and quickly. No one has conclusively been able to find the determining factor that makes some people somnambulists. This ability can appear regardless of sex, intelligence, race or occupation. (Note: in stage-hypnosis shows, the entertainer looks for the somnambulists in the audience!)

A similar percentage of the population appears to be unable to reach anything but a light trance. Light trance, however, is all that is necessary for past-life regression to work. The majority of people fall somewhere between these two extremes. Most of them are capable of reaching a somnambulistic state eventually, but the hypnotist needs to take longer to aid them in getting to that level. For these individuals, the brain doesn't spontaneously leap to great trance depths; it usually requires repeat sessions. Practice is necessary. Because of this, there are past-life regressionists who prefer to have their clients book several sessions, for the more frequently a person is hypnotized, the deeper that person will be able to go.

Generally, people who are in hypnosis, whether it's a light or deep trance, remain physically immobile during the entire session. Apart from that, everyone has a unique response to being hypnotized. Many people discover that their body temperature drops during the session, so I always have a basket of comforters handy for snuggling.

Sometimes people I'm hypnotizing tell me that they feel as though they are floating above their bodies. Some state that they feel expanded, or even distorted, as though their arms are reversed or in different places than they actually are. Others have the sensation of heaviness in their limbs. Tingling or numbness may also be experienced. A few have told me that they feel as though they have shrunk in size and become extremely tiny. Others, especially in their first several sessions, remain perfectly aware of every sensation and every small sound in the room; they simply relax.

Just as when we sleep, fluctuation in the depth of trance is normal. It's like riding through a hilly region. At one moment, one is at the crest of a hill, and at the next moment descends to the valley floor. Individuals will say things like, *"I was really deep. Then for some reason, it seemed like I woke up for awhile, and then I went back even deeper."*

There are two comments that I hear over and over after a person I've hypnotized emerges and opens her or his eyes. The first is, *"That was really relaxing!"* The second is, *"Wow! That felt weird."* The first response comes from people who experienced light to medium trance. The second, which is always a pleasant exclamation, comes from those who went to a greater depth. Both are capable of experiencing a past-life regression.

Here's how hypnosis feels to me: When I am hypnotized, at first I am kind of drowsy and even a little bit itchy. It takes a few minutes for me to settle down into relaxation. After a period of time, my limbs start to feel incredibly heavy and immobile, although not uncomfortably so. When I go to a very deep state, this heaviness either becomes more intense or I lose awareness of my body completely, while my mind seems to be more open and flexible. I become so immersed in my inner state that I don't bother to note what is happening around me. If, for example, a lawn mower were to buzz outside or a furnace were to turn on, I wouldn't pay any attention.

I've hypnotized people who have gone to such an intensely focused level that they have remained undisturbed even through the extreme noise of a police helicopter directly overhead, or a sea-plane landing only a few yards away, or a siren from a fire station in the next building going off! Yet, these people could have easily responded to any emergency taking place in their immediate environment.

It is typical to experience a deep and pleasant physical relaxation during hypnosis. This can make people feel fuzzy for a few minutes after emerging, just like one feels after awaking in the morning, or walking up the aisle of a movie theater after a good film.

People sometimes ask whether hypnosis and meditation are the same thing. They are very similar states, except that in hypnosis, we concentrate our attention in a very focused way, excluding everything else that is going on, while in meditation we are generally more open to receiving impressions and have a less restricted agenda. Henry Leo Bolduc likens meditation to looking through a telescope, while hypnosis is like looking through a microscope.

BRAIN WAVE CYCLES

CYCLES PER SECOND	STATE AND DESCRIPTION
Above 28	HIGH ANXIETY
14-28	BETA (Normal Alert Consciousness)
7-14	ALPHA (Light Trance: able to recall past lives)
4-7	THETA (Deep Trance: past-life memories more vivid)
.5-4	DELTA (Sleep)
Below 0	DEATH

BRAIN WAVES AND
PAST-LIFE MEMORIES

ೞ

There are four basic patterns of brainwave cycles: Beta, Alpha, Theta and Delta. Because they were named in order of discovery, they are not in alphabetical order.

Beta is the level of active, wide-awake consciousness where our brain-wave cycles per second are fairly rapid. We are in Beta when we do things like think hard about a problem, study, make judgments, discern, analyze, and organize information. *Delta* occurs when we are asleep. The two patterns in between wakefulness and sleep, *Alpha* and *Theta,* are associated with hypnosis.

For past-life recollection, we allow the cycle of brain waves to slow down a little from alert consciousness, bringing the mind to the state called *Alpha.* Alpha is equivalent to a mild hypnotic state. This is the same brain-wave level we are in when we are absorbed in a good book, or lost in thought. Most of us go in and out of Alpha many times a day without even realizing it. You might even be in Alpha right now! People are often surprised at how easy and natural it is for memories to bubble up while they are in Alpha.

To give an example of what this stage of hypnosis feels like, imagine that you are at the movie theater watching a suspense film while a man sitting next to you is eating popcorn. At some level of your mind, you smell and hear the popcorn and see the motion of the man's arm moving to his mouth, yet you are largely unaware of this because your attention and emotions are riveted on the suspenseful action on the screen. This is similar to the way the mind operates in the Alpha state of hypnosis.

Theta is a deeper level of hypnosis where the number of brain-wave cycles per second slows down even more. This level is where somnambulism occurs. Some of the most profound past-life regression work is done in this state. Like Alpha, the *Theta* state is also very comfortable and natural. Individuals in Theta become very absorbed in their regression and experience remembered events much more vividly than those in Alpha.

Some interesting studies have shown that during a past-life regression there is often a mixture of brain-wave patterns, with some brain waves at very deep levels and others at the level of alert, awake consciousness.

HOW WILL MY PAST LIFE COME TO ME WHEN I'M IN HYPNOSIS?

⳨

There are multiple ways in which people remember their past lives during hypnosis. In my own experiences, sometimes after being hypnotized I have had lifetimes that spontaneously flooded into my mind of their own accord, unfolding easily like a drama. In others, I've only received information after being asked questions by the hypnotist. Those whom I help to regress similarly have a great deal of variety in their experiences of past-life regression. There is no one-size-fits-all!

It is common for people to retain awareness both of their past and their current lifetimes during their regression, with a foot in each world. They are equally the main character and the observer.

At other times, they literally become the person they were in their past life. Their speech, expressions and mannerisms completely change. On several occasions, clients have actually begun speaking in another language and I have had to remind them to speak to me English!

Some individuals receive only a small, brief glimpse of one of their past lives, as though the curtain of memory has opened for just a split second and then quickly closed again. It is much like having a long, complex dream, but remembering only one tiny fragment. If examined carefully, that snippet of memory usually provides a rich understanding, and is often exactly what the person needed.

This was what occurred to me when I had my very first

past-life memory. I was with a group of people who were being regressed for fun by an amateur to see if any of us could recollect a lifetime associated with the great pyramids of Giza in Egypt. Our leader was inexpert, and nothing was coming into my mind, so I just permitted myself to tune out of the chatter about pyramids and drift without expectation, enjoying the relaxation. After about ten minutes of such drifting, a memory suddenly popped into my head out of the blue.

I was the mother of a boy. He was about ten years old, dressed in a tunic, and he had a terrible, incessant condition where his body would convulse in huge, jolting spasms. There was nothing I could do to help. I had such enormous empathy for him that I felt every convulsion he experienced. My heart suffered greatly for my son.

This memory was phenomenally vivid. For just a split second, I *was* that woman. I experienced all the powerful emotions of this mother, who was very different from the person I am today—and yet it came in such a sudden flash that it occurred much faster than it has taken me to write this paragraph! As soon as the memory was over, the emotions accompanying it dissolved and I was left with a puzzling snippet.

Even with such a tiny fragment and without consciously thinking about it, I instantly recognized who the boy was, someone I know in a completely different context today. Later, I also realized the big lesson I have learned since that lifetime: that of detached compassion. Whereas in that life I was unable to separate my feelings from my son's pain, in my present lifetime I have always had an instinctive ability to empathize with my loved ones and clients, while remaining in a separate and safe place, and not "taking on their stuff."

This little bit of a memory has remained very precious to me.

Over the years it has explained many things about my life and my relationship with the person who had then been my son, as well as my responses to people who are in trouble.

The experiences you have during past-life regression will be similarly unique and varied. It is important to keep an open mind about the process.

THE ROLE OF OUR (FIVE) SENSES

CR

While we once limited our senses to five, adding perhaps the sixth sense of intuition, we are now beginning to realize that we possess many more senses than we previously believed. Humans have, for example, an innate sense of balance, and a sense of knowing where they are in reference to other objects sharing their space. Thirst is a separate sense, as is sexual desire. For ease of understanding, in this chapter when speaking of the senses, we will refer primarily to the basic five senses, also adding emotion and/or intuition.

In our human bodies, the only way in which we can experience and perceive life is through our senses. When we are forming or remembering images with our inner mind, we similarly use the same five senses. One or two of these senses is generally predominant when we enter our inner minds, and it is different with each individual.

EXPERIMENT ONE

1. *Close your eyes and picture a red barn on a farm. See it as clearly as possible.*

2. *Now add to your picture the sound of cows mooing...*

3. *Add the taste of fresh, creamy milk, or whipped cream...*

4. *Add the feelings of scratchy bales of hay and rough barn boards...*

5. *And now add the smells of manure and alfalfa.*

Notice how each added sense enhances and expands the image of the barn, and makes it more realistic. Probably some of the senses were easier for you to imagine than others.

UP UNTIL RECENTLY, hypnotists and past-life regressionists would commonly instruct their clients to *visualize* scenes when conducting a past-life regression. They used expressions like, "*See* what is going on around you. *Look at* what is happening." They would rarely include the other four senses.

We have learned, however, that limiting the focus of a past-life exploration to sight alone and disregarding the other senses creates problems for a certain percentage of the population. While the large majority of the people have no difficulty seeing pictures with their eyes closed, some individuals are completely unable to do this. They cannot see at all with their inner minds. There are others who can visualize a little bit, but the pictures are not vivid or clear, and they must strain to do so.

Even for those who can visualize easily, using the sense of sight exclusively in a regression is limiting. In the same way that imagining the barn became more real when you added other sensations, so a past-life regression can become more vivid by opening to all of the senses. Information comes through in a much more satisfactory way when we mix and match our senses to remember and relive the stories of our deep past. Adding our emotional responses—our feelings—to the image further refines the memories.

TO OFFER YOU an idea of how your five senses might work when you experience a past-life regression, do the following exercise:

EXPERIMENT TWO

This is an easy exercise about remembering your own bed at home. Read one step at a time, close your eyes and follow the instructions you have just read.

1. *[See] What does your bed look like? Look at the light and shadow on your bed, and see the colors and details.*

2. *[Touch] How does the support of your bed feel under your body when you curl up under the cov-*

ers? How do the blankets and sheets feel against your skin? What does your head feel like on the pillow?

3. *[Smell] Imagine what your sheets and pillow smell like when they have been freshly washed. Smell the scents of your blankets and bedroom, and notice any characteristic fragrances on your body as you rest in your bed, like soap or cologne.*

4. *[Taste] Imagine that you are lying in bed eating your favorite snack, or, if you prefer, that you have just brushed your teeth. Taste the flavors on the inside of your mouth.*

5. *[Hear] Listen for the sounds you hear when you are in your bed. Are there birds outside, or traffic, or the hum of a furnace? What sounds do you hear when you move under the covers, or when you pull a blanket up?*

6. *[Feel] Recall a time when you slept deeply, and how extraordinarily good that felt.*

Which senses worked the best for you in the above exercise? Which were the most difficult to access? Usually we have one or two senses that are predominant, and a few that aren't as easy for us. Everyone is a little different in how they remember.

RECALLING A PAST life can be as simple as remembering your bed! The trick to more vivid recollection is to involve all five senses, as well as the feelings (emotions) and/or intuitions.

VISUALIZATION

Were you able to see your bed easily? If so, you are visual, like the large majority of people. Visual people can see clear pictures when recalling past lives. For some, visions of their past incarnations appear in vivid and complete cinematic detail. Such people often remark during their regression that it is like watching a movie being played right before their eyes. Others report that they see pictures, but these pictures unfold gradually, often only after questions are asked.

When I am working with a visual person, I usually begin the past-life regression by asking her to look down at her feet. Then I suggest that she gradually lift her eyes and expand her field of vision to include more and more glimpses of what her body looks like and what is around her.

A few visually oriented people never see pictures of the entire scene; instead, their inner sight rests upon just one detail at a time, such as a person's face, or a tree, or a piece of lace on a cuff. If a visual person is self-conscious about being regressed, she might find that her visualizations are a little bit vague at first, until she becomes accustomed to the process.

Many visual people can easily picture themselves as they looked in their past lives. It is as though they are standing outside of their bodies and watching themselves. Others may visualize the scene around them well, but never see themselves clearly. For them, the process is more like looking through the eyes of their former selves.

THE OTHER SENSES

Those who have trouble visualizing generally find that one or more of their other senses proves to be a more accessible doorway for accessing past-life experiences. Some of these individuals report that they experience a powerful sense of touch with their eyes closed. Such people are primarily kinesthetic. While they may not be able to see what they are wearing on their feet during a past-life regression, they might feel the texture of footwear against their skin, notice the sensation of the ground under their feet, or feel aches or muscle tension in their feet and ankles.

People who hear well during regressions are auditory. Musicians often fall into this category. They are keenly aware of sounds. When they are perceiving a scene in trance, it is easy for them to listen to sounds like the voices of people speaking, music being played, or the harmonies of nature. Once in a while, a highly auditory person will actually hear a story being dictated, as if another voice is telling it to them.

A select few people are primarily gustatory or olfactory. Their senses of taste and smell are incredibly refined and powerful when having a past-life regression. Such individuals might find that the scents or tastes of a scene, such as spices in a marketplace, animals in a stable, or food consumed at mealtimes, are their best pathway to remembering.

Emotions are predominant for some people. A man might not have a clear vision of a past life, but he may suddenly experience overwhelming sorrow during a regression and recognize from the emotion that his child has just died; or he may find himself laughing, and through that emotion remember that he was a merchant enjoying the company of his friends at a feast.

Finally, a percentage of people simply have a sense, a know-ingness, of what is unfolding. An example would be that of a client of mine who said, *"I don't see or feel anything, but for some reason, I just know that I am living in the mountains of Peru."* Such people intuit, rather than directly experience, what is going on.

EXPERIMENT THREE

This is a pleasurable gustatory and olfactory experiment. Please do not do it if it distresses you in any way; enjoy this one!

1. *After closing your eyes, remember and savor the taste of your favorite candy when you were a young child.*

2. *Now close your eyes again and remember the fragrance of the cologne or hand lotion that your mother or one of your favorite adults wore when you were very young.*

FEW PEOPLE ARE limited to just one sense. Most of us can successfully use combinations of some, or even all, the senses to receive our impressions of past lives, just as we do in our present-day life. Be aware that people may re-experience their past lives through senses that were acute in *that lifetime*, even though that may not be their dominant sense today! For instance, someone with normally excellent hearing may go back to a lifetime when she was deaf.

During a regression, if one sense isn't coming through clearly—say, for example, it is difficult to see a clear picture of what is on your feet—becoming aware of another avenue will be helpful, such as feeling what you are wearing on your feet or listening for the sound of your footsteps. (You could also smell your feet, I suppose, although I haven't yet had a client do that!)

A WOMAN NAMED Jennifer came to me for past-life regression to find the source of a particular life issue. She described herself as being highly visual, and this was borne out by testing that I did with her. When Jennifer was regressed and guided to go to the former point in time when her issues began, disappointment clouded her brow. Still in hypnosis, she blurted out, *"This isn't working. I can't see a thing."*

We persisted, however, and Jennifer began to explore her other senses, as well as her emotions. Upon doing that, the recognition suddenly came to her that she was in her mother's womb. This was why she couldn't see anything! The information that followed provided exactly the insights she needed for healing her issue.

I WANT TO EXPERIENCE PAST-LIFE REGRESSION, BUT I WORRY THAT I MIGHT REMEMBER HORRIBLE THINGS

CR

While people do sometimes remember horrible past-life events during regressions, in my experience it has always been a relief for them to do so. Such memories inevitably offer them great freedom and release. More about this will be covered in the chapter on how past-life regression can heal.

A skilled past-life regression therapist knows how to word suggestions so that an individual will not experience any unnecessary suffering, fear or panic, and has been trained to handle such emotionally charged situations, should they arise. If someone appears to be stuck in an uncomfortable setting during a past-life regression, the option I usually offer is that they can fast-forward, as though fast-forwarding a DVD or a video, until they have moved beyond the event. It can also easily be suggested that the person distance himself or herself from the scene, as though they are sitting in a theater, watching a movie about someone else.

Although it is true that we may have been seriously impacted by traumas and trying events in our past lives, keep in mind that most lifetimes are a mixture of both happy and sad experiences, even as your life is today. Those with whom I have worked have had many joyous memories. Laughing out loud, smiling, and experiencing sensations of emotional warmth and love are as common as tears during regression sessions.

Reliving and relieving our painful memories is only one aspect of past-life regression, and one, as you will discover, which can be incredibly healing. You may also have a session in which you remember a pleasant lifetime! Perhaps you had a beautiful relationship, an attribute, or a talent that would be useful for you to recall today. That is a wonderful way to experience past-life regression, and can be very fruitful indeed.

> *Jason went back to a lifetime as a happy young boy in ancient times. He lived in a city which had build-ings and huge staircases made out of massive stone blocks. These were supposed to be very holy places, which people of the time treated with great awe and sanctity. The boy, however, would skip and run over the stones with gleeful irreverence when no one was watching.*
>
> *When he was older, he used to serve food and drink to the populace as the ancient equivalent of a bartender. He was very popular, for he had comical gifts, and his antics would always make people laugh.*

As a result of this memory, Jason, who was quite serious, was reminded of inner qualities of levity and humor that had long been suppressed.

> *Sarah had the simple but special memory of being a Chinese man who spent his days in a country setting, where he happily worked on calligraphy and delicate art projects. Sarah had always been very attracted to Oriental artwork, and now understood why. The ses-sion aroused a renewed interest to use drawing and painting as a way of relieving tension.*

SOMETIMES EVENTS THAT might seem traumatic to others are not interpreted that way by the individual being regressed. Such a memory came from a session with Sean.

> Sean regressed to a lifetime that occurred in ancient Greece or Rome. To his amazement, he found himself wearing the robes of a philosopher. He was gazing upon a statue that had been erected in his honor. Tears both of happiness and humility filled his eyes as he reflected upon the fame others had bestowed upon him. He was a simple, highly intelligent, and very ethical man.
>
> At the end of his life, the same public who at one time idolized him turned on him, and he was executed for refusing to recant certain beliefs. Normally one would expect that such an execution would be a shattering incident to remember, but this was not the case with the philosopher. He recognized why it was happening and did not feel any ill will, sense of persecution, or resentment which would carry over into future lifetimes. His death in that incarnation, although sad and regrettable, was actually a serene experience, for he had been, overall, a happy person.

In discussing the regression afterwards, Sean's focus was on the positive aspects of the remembered life. The mode of death was incidental to him. He revealed that he had never before felt such unadulterated joy as that which he experienced during the regression to his former life.

SOMETIMES DURING A past-life regression, people will mask, deny, or gloss over trauma. This can happen for a variety of reasons. Such an individual will have an experience very different from Sean's. They may retrieve an incarnation that appears to be uneventful, but which has certain gaps of time where they do not remember what happened. These blank spaces may be accompanied either by a niggling sense that something unpleasant may have occurred, or by a dissatisfaction upon emerging from the session. Another way of masking is when a person goes through dreadful memories, but shows a cool detachment from the events that he or she is re-experiencing. Usually such a person will show no strong emotion at all during the regression, regardless of whether the scenes are happy or sad.

It could be that the person is not yet ready to deal with the trauma and begin the mending process. In such instances, for healing and release to take place the individual may need to reexperience the lifetime more than once. Often it is only when we return several times to a past event that the whole story, with all its attendant emotions, will emerge.

> *Abigail regressed to a lifetime centuries ago in Europe where she was accused of being a witch and burned at the stake. Her memories were devoid of emotion and she related the story in a very cool and uninvolved way. It was only after several regressions to the same lifetime that strong emotions from that incident and its attendant repercussions on her present life began to emerge.*

Our innermost selves are very wise, and will only bring to the surface that which we can handle at a given time.

CAN I SOLVE ALL MY PROBLEMS IN ONE PAST-LIFE SESSION?

∞

Yes...maybe.

For the majority of us, however, truly effective work entails a commitment to past-life regression therapy involving multiple sessions. As with any other meditative or trance state, past-life regression becomes easier the more one delves into it. It is like a muscle that performs better with practice. While it is not uncommon for people to access profound memories immediately, others have a few cold starts before they warm up to the experience and really take off!

In my own journey, I waited for years before having a one-on-one past-life regression. When it finally occurred, all that I got out of the session, which lasted for several hours, were a few glimpses of a dull and rather bitter lifetime as a peasant. I was doubtful that the little bits of memory I had were even real.

My expectations of what a past-life regression was going to feel like and what the results would be were extremely different from what actually happened, which is one of the reasons I am writing this book. I'd mistakenly believed that I would be in a deep kind of stupor, and that I would somehow automatically be transported into the maelstrom of a previous lifetime, one which would explain and heal all of my problems.

Sometimes that is the way it goes, but that wasn't at all what happened to me, and I was disappointed. Relying upon only one highly charged and melodramatic regression to retrieve, relive, and release one's pent-up and deepest issues places a lot of pressure on a person to perform. This can definitely be a hindrance to the process.

For past-life regression therapy to be fully effective, we need to explore all of the roots of our negative patterns. *Nearly always, we will find multiple lifetimes connected to a troublesome problem.*

Each lifetime offers its own unique contribution to understanding and releasing the issue. We are naturally more inclined to access memories where we were the "good guy" or the victim than those in which we were the villain. Often, however, the deepest healing occurs when we uncover our more sordid lifetimes, those where we made a limiting decision or did some kind of harm which perpetuated the chain of events that is now so bewildering to us. Such lifetimes do not always readily surface until a person has become comfortable with past-life regression, and is ready to face her or his own deepest truth. This takes time, persistence, and trust.

It is laughable to think of seeing a traditional therapist and resolving one's issues in a single session. While past-life regression is a much faster and incredibly effective process, for the majority of people multiple sessions are the best way to find all the missing pieces of the puzzle.

RETURNING TO THE
SAME LIFETIME

಄

In past-life therapy, an individual may experience a different life-time in each session, or he might regress repeatedly to the same lifetime. When that happens, each regression offers additional insights and information. Sometimes a soul can only absorb a small chunk of a previous life, and needs time to assimilate and digest before it can continue with more. Each past-life experience offers only what the individual is able to handle at that moment in time.

Quite a few years ago, I received a rich fragment from an important past-life. In this brief glimpse, I was a wise and seasoned commander of legions in ancient Rome. Although I could not discover his name or exact rank, I tuned into the flavor, the stoicism and the wisdom of this powerful man of long ago, who loved and lived for Rome. Over time, I thought about him and his character quite a bit.

Several years later, in response to a past-life regression quest where I hoped to understand a friendship that had soured, the lifetime that came up was of the same Roman commander. As I began the regression, I found myself having recently been appointed to a new, prestigious post of command. I was impatiently awaiting the completion of my armor so that I could assume my new title. It was gorgeous, intricately detailed armor. When the magnificent helmet was placed before me, in my present-day observer mind I imagined picking it up and putting it on my head—but, to my surprise, that action was immediately halted! It seemed that there was a slave who had the job of doing that. It would be bad etiquette for someone in my position to put on his own helmet.

The armor was very hot and heavy. He/I immediately made up my mind that anything I perceived as physical discomfort would simply make me stronger, and would spur me on to greater endurance and determination. Although the information was interesting, nothing in that regression pertained to my problematic friendship, and I felt frustrated that my question remained unanswered.

After several more years, I was being hypnotized by a student when I spontaneously regressed to a third experience in the lifetime of the same Roman commander. In this session, many more details of his life emerged. I noted the way I would ride in a chariot in front of the adoring crowds, with a skilled charioteer guiding the horses, and my philosophical observations of the way the masses of people behaved towards their leaders.

I found myself on bended knee in a small temple, sincerely presenting an offering to the megalithic statue of a goddess whom I worshipped. I noted details about the interior of my home, where I was rarely present... and then I explored my relationship with my wife.

Although she had married me for status and fed off my fame and fortune, she was genuinely devoted to me. Her entire life centered around me. I, however, had no interest in her. While I remained courteous, I was remote and rejecting.

The pattern was resoundingly like that of the soured friendship I'd earlier questioned, although this time around I had found myself quite deservedly on the receiving end. It was karmic justice. My answer had finally come. Although it seemed to be several years late, the truth was that it didn't arrive until I could believe, understand, accept and integrate it.

WILL I REMEMBER DYING?

☙

At the end of every remembered lifetime, I guide my clients to the circumstances and events surrounding their remembered death. Because of the precise way I word it—*"Now go to the circumstances and events surrounding your death in the lifetime you are now remembering"*—they are able to view the death scene thoroughly and yet objectively. I have never once regressed an individual who has resisted investigating her or his remembered death, or who had a bad experience doing so, regardless of the form in which death came. On the contrary, this process is almost inevitably a relief and offers a sense of completion.

Because of the wording I use, which was suggested to me by the highly respected past-life regressionist Henry Leo Bolduc, my clients avoid getting immersed in physical pain. Occasionally a person will have a glimmer of the sensations of dying, such as the burn of a bullet or the feeling of congested lungs. Should they appear to be struggling, I simply move them forward quickly to the point where their soul leaves the body and they inevitably enter a state of peace.

There is quite a bit of variety in the ways in which people relate having died. I am often very surprised. While some were murdered or fell victim to accidents, the majority of death experiences I have heard have been quite natural. Much of the time, people do not really know how to describe the cause of their death, nor do they offer any medical diagnosis. They relate that they were "just sick" or old. To me, this is further evidence of the credibility of past-life remembrances, for most people in times past didn't even have access to physicians, let alone specific diagnoses of their conditions.

I always ask my clients to share the last thought they have just before the death of the body, and then ask what their impressions are immediately upon leaving the body. Many people report hovering above the scene and looking down upon themselves.

> *Jacob regressed to an incarnation in the Middle East where he traveled with a group of avid, philosophical young men who preached and sought social change. He was arrested and killed by being thrown off a high city wall. When I asked what his impressions were after leaving his body, he said that he could see himself lying on the ground. He expressed pity for his friends, for as he looked back down upon his form, he saw that his limbs were broken and very twisted from the fall. According to the religious conventions of the time, his friends would be obliged to straighten out his body before burying him and it was going to be a difficult task.*

In my experience, only a few individuals who died with unfinished business or a lot of guilt have expressed any kind of sense of disturbance after their deaths, and even they were eventually brought to a more comfortable space.

> *Brad, the man who had been disemboweled and then torn apart after being chained to horses, reported what his impressions were immediately after he left that tortured form. He said that he could see the remains of his body lying in a field, and then he began to cry. "The horses knew," he said sorrowfully. "They knew, and they didn't want to do it."*

Most people relate having a sense of enormous peace and relief after remembering the experience of dying during a past-life regression. When taken to the point where the spirit leaves the body, it is not unusual for them to describe a sense of drifting upwards or even to report seeing a tunnel.

There is a surprising elegance and reassurance in remembering the natural process of dying and re-experiencing what happens to the soul afterwards.

PATTERNS

ॐ

All of us have particular themes and patterns in our lives. When we explore our history through past-life regression, we sometimes find that these patterns have been repeated over and over and over again, lifetime after lifetime. Our patterns may be centuries old. They may have become so familiar that we have grown comfortable with them. Certain patterns are etched so deeply upon our being that we may scarcely be aware they exist. It is as if we are running on automatic.

Past-life patterns are as varied as the people who experience them. They may emerge as disproportionate emotions, inexplicable attachments, obsessions, natural talents, physical ailments, unusual fears or other perplexing manifestations that cannot readily be explained. One may have had a pattern of multiple lifetimes in which she did not stick up for herself; another may find that he was a soldier in life after life, either killing or being killed in battle; yet another may discover a pattern of repeated self-indulgent and destructive behavior.

Our past-life patterns are not necessarily negative. Some patterns are positive, and serve a person well. Examples of positive patterns from previous lifetimes might include attributes like having an innate and easy sense of humor, possessing natural musical talent, or being an instinctive healer.

Jane, a woman who has natural healing gifts, discovered multiple lifetimes in an assortment of different societies where she repeatedly had the role of helping people in medicinal or intuitive ways.

Some of our patterns are simply neutral. Neutral patterns provide us with interesting personality traits, but don't affect our lives tremendously. Examples of neutral patterns might include a person who has developed the trait of being a good listener, someone who likes being by the sea, or an individual who enjoys noticing the fine details of intricate artwork.

What usually draw our attention, of course, are the less fortunate patterns we possess, the ones which are filled with negativity and unhappiness. Often these negative patterns don't make any sense and defy analysis. We may find ourselves repeating and replaying bewildering emotions that are not relevant to our current situation, or being the victim of the same set of circumstances over and over again.

An indicator that a past life pattern might be involved in a life issue occurs when we find ourselves saying things like:

- *"Oh, no! Not again!" "I can't understand why I feel this way; it's not logical."*

- *"No matter how hard I try, I always attract the same type of person."*

- *"Why does _____ [fill in the blank] always happen to me?"*

The worst of these negative patterns disrupt the flow of our lives and demand that we do something to repair the situation. Such patterns often stem from the unwanted residue of former lifetimes, stubbornly clinging to our energy fields in snarled tangles.

ME, A PERP?!

One pattern that frequently emerges in past-life regression work is that of being a victim. A high percentage of the people with whom I work discover that they were victimized and persecuted in some manner lifetime after lifetime. There are usually themes to their patterns that they unwillingly seem to magnetize over and over again, such as a wise healer who is violently persecuted out of fear (e.g., a witch burned at the stake), or an individual who is repeatedly abandoned by parents/lovers/friends, or a person who ends up being outcast or imprisoned because of a misunderstanding. Victimization frequently turns out to be an entrenched and sad pattern that has replayed itself over many lifetimes.

If we are brave enough to dig deeply, those of us who have had past lives of being victims will nearly always discover the terrible truth: at some point we were also perpetrators. This is not easy material to unearth, nor does it come forth readily from the subconscious. It takes great maturity and self-honesty to face the awful things we may have done that have set the wheel of suffering in motion.

> Jamie, who had been molested in her present life, discovered through past-life regression that she had suffered molestation in previous lives as well. Eventually she uncovered a lifetime where she herself had been a molester.

Finding such a key event offers a powerful opportunity for relief and release. It also provides us with the opportunity to take full responsibility for all aspects of our lives.

Most people are not ready to see themselves as perpetrators or wrongdoers unless they are also at the level in their soul development where they may finally heal through the miraculous process of forgiving and accepting forgiveness. The good news is that there is always a point at which a debt may be considered paid, and a time when the soul may finally be free to move out of bondage to new experiences.

Nothing that occurs to us or to anyone else is random.

THE POWER OF CHOICE

The choices we have made in past incarnations are particularly powerful and dominant in our larger tapestry. Our choices are like sacred promises to our souls. Although we forget from lifetime to lifetime that we have made them, these vows from the past remain within our energy patterns. They are responsible for some of our automatic, unthinking behavior.

Remember Jean, the woman who was regressed to a lifetime as a male slave in the South? His many years as a slave were very uneventful. He had been treated decently, and died peacefully at an old age. The key remembrance from that lifetime of slavery occurred one day as he stood in a field looking at the distant horizon. He realized that he would never be free. He resigned himself to his circumstances, and made a powerful decision: from then on, no matter what was before him, he would always do the best job he could.

While this is not a dramatic illustration, it is powerful. Jean revealed that this particular ethic, that of doing the best she could regardless of her circumstances, was a deeply engrained and propelling factor in her present life, but up until her regression she had not been consciously aware of it. Recognizing both the positive pattern and its origins gave her a great sense of satisfaction.

Lucy was attracted to a man in her office. From the moment she first laid eyes on him, she felt an instant attraction and a strong sense of familiarity, even though he wasn't particularly handsome or charismat-

ic. In regression Lucy discovered that in a past lifetime she and the man had been very happily married, and she had made a vow. She swore to her husband that she would always recognize him and love him, even after death when they were in heaven. A part of Lucy's soul continued to honor that promise, although it was no longer appropriate.

There is great wisdom in traditional Western wedding vows, where couples pledge to love one another "till death us do part"!

EACH LIFETIME WE experience offers us choices, and those choices help set our patterns in motion. A decision made by a man in Medieval Italy to marry for money might create a present-day consequence in which he finds himself relentlessly entangled in superficial circumstances. A choice made by a woman in ancient China to risk her life to help starving orphans might result today in her repeatedly having someone show up to rescue her when she is in need.

Every choice that we make in a past life has a strong effect on what happens to us in the future.

ANOTHER ASPECT OF past lives which adds its imprint to the design of our soul is the way in which we have responded to situations and experiences, especially when those responses which were anchored in emotion. Even though our choices in such instances may seem less deliberate, they are also involved in these reactions. Our past responses can become anchored and turn into knee-jerk reactions to present-life situations which defy understanding until we go back to the past to dig up and expose their roots.

Heather wanted a past-life regression because she was confused about her relationship with her husband. He was a good man and treated her well. She found him attractive, yet she felt a sense of revulsion at his sexual advances. In Heather's regression, she went back to a harsh life in the American West in the 1800s. Abandoned at a young age, and having no resources, she was offered employment in a brothel in a saloon. The thought of prostituting herself upset her. Yet, she chose to go ahead because she felt she didn't have any other options and would otherwise starve. It was a brutal and difficult life for her, and she hated the coarse men with whom she had sex for money. Sexuality became inextricably linked with revulsion, and turned into an instinctive pattern that persisted long after the cause had disappeared.

UNRESOLVED ISSUES

One of the most indelible imprints from our past lives occurs when something from our past never has the chance to become fully resolved. It's as though we have remained stuck in a time warp. A portion of our psyche continues to attempt to deal with the ancient problem, even though the triggering event has long since disappeared.

Energy that is needed to function in a healthy and happy way on a day-to-day level is instead redirected and consumed by these unsolved blocks. On an unconscious level, we continue to manifest circumstances that bring back these old puzzling issues over and over again.

Justina, a healthy, happily married young woman came to me for hypnosis because she couldn't stop overeating, in spite of years of dieting and an otherwise common-sense attitude towards her habits. No matter how much food was in her stomach, she always felt insistently hungry.

In one of Justina's weight-management sessions, she decided to undergo a past-life regression. She found herself wandering alone as a thin, weak little boy on the streets of a European city in the late 1700s. She was from the lower classes, and her parents had died. There was no adult to care for her and, neglected, she starved to death. Justina realized that her present-day compulsive overeating was linked to the hunger of the child, which had never been satisfied.

TRAUMATIC OR IMPACTING EVENTS

A bizarre phobia, an illogical terror or a frustrating pattern that has no reasonable explanation can be an indicator of a possible past-life condition that has leaked into the present day. Such an issue will often persist despite all efforts to stop it. These patterns may be linked to traumatic, startling, or otherwise unpleasant events that occurred in past lives. A man who fell overboard and drowned at sea in a past lifetime might be afraid of the water; a woman who was burned in a tragic fire might feel nervous around fireplaces.

When Laura consulted with me, she related that she had been having panic attacks for years. Doctors had prescribed medication, to no avail. She would frequently wake up in the middle of the night full of terror, sweating, her heart pounding, although there had been no precipitating dream or event of which she was aware. Abdominal pain would often accompany these night terrors. She wondered if past-life regression could help.

After being hypnotized, Laura had three regressions in succession. In the first, she regressed to very primitive times. She remembered being a man who was suddenly killed when an unknown assailant thrust a spear into his abdomen. In the second regression, she was a young and frightened sailor on a sailing vessel in wartime. In the midst of much pandemonium on the ship, he was surprised when something—possibly a cannon—suddenly exploded, hit him in the abdomen and killed him.

In the final regression, Laura found herself to be a

*middle-aged bald man named Harry, living in the early
1900s in England. Harry worked in an office, and was
married to an extremely unstable and angry woman.
One night while he slept, his psychotic wife killed him
in his sleep, probably stabbing him in the abdomen.
Harry he died in pain, but it happened too suddenly for
him to be completely aware of the instrument which
was used. No one ever found out that he had been
murdered.*

More than two years later, I checked back with Laura and
asked how she was. She reported that she had experienced one
very minor incident of panic the day after her regression, and
since then has been free of the incidents that used to hold her
hostage.

*Caleb was a young man who regressed to a primitive
lifetime many ages ago, when he lived with a tribe in
a mountainous area that may have been somewhere
in northern Europe. Wolves were a constant threat to
his people. In a very serious attack, a pack of wolves
mauled his leg and nearly killed him, but he survived.
In that same lifetime, a girl with whom he was in love
failed to meet him for a rendezvous and apparently
disappeared. He never found out what happened to
her. Only in his life review did he learn that she had
been killed by wolves.*

In our discussion after his session, Caleb revealed that he
had physical problems with the leg that had been mauled in his
remembered lifetime. He was also unreasonably afraid of dogs.

As a child, I used to be terrified whenever a small plane would fly over our house at night. I never talked with an adult about my fear; I assumed that everyone was equally afraid of airplanes. It was only when I accessed my previous life during World War II that this childhood terror made perfect sense.

TALENTS AND ATTRIBUTES

Kimberly came to see me fully expecting to experience a traumatic regression. Instead, she went back in time to a pleasant former life in Ireland where she had sung in pubs. As a result of her session, she became interested in singing, and within a year had begun booking engagements as a singer in coffee houses and clubs.

Our past abilities and gifts can continue in our current lives. It is exciting when a client is reminded of a talent or other gift. For some, it is like unlocking the door to a room filled with long-forgotten treasure.

A musical prodigy like a Mozart, a child who is a mathematical genius, or an exceptional and instinctive athlete undoubtedly developed those skills in a former lifetime.

LEARNED LESSONS

It is not just our gifts, like an ability to paint or to do well in sports, which may be linked to our past lives. Our attributes of character have similarly been developed in other lifetimes.

Parents of large families will often attest to the fact that, even as babies, their children demonstrate vastly different traits. Some people find it easy to avoid addictions; others don't seem to know how to stop. Some people are frugal with their money; others are wasteful. Some people have an innate ability to communicate with animals; others fear and dislike animals. Anything that we have developed in another lifetime, particularly as a matter of choice and struggle, is a quality we get to keep.

> Guillermo was the courageous young man mentioned earlier in this book who had been able to rise from adversity and take on a strong leadership role. He was from a Hispanic family, had no acting ability and was not adept at speaking other languages, much less mimicking accents. Yet, when he was regressed, he immediately began speaking in a thick hillbilly dialect, marked by poor grammar and quaint slang expressions. He said that his last name was Pritchard.

> He lived on a farm in the United States in the 1800s, and was an uncomplicated, simple person. As a boy, his favorite pastimes were rolling a hoop with a stick and chasing chickens in the yard. The highlight of his life was his marriage to his sweetheart. Then the Civil War broke out and he joined the Union army, where he eventually became a captain.

In a harrowing battle which he described vividly, Pritchard's leg was badly injured. In spite of this, he chose to ignore his own pain and crawled through the battlefield, putting his life in jeopardy to save a number of injured men by pulling them out of harm's way. Later, his leg was amputated in a gruesome operation. Although he nearly died, he survived and went home on crutches, only to find that his beloved wife had died while he was away.

During his life review at the conclusion of the regression, Guillermo recognized that Pritchard's acts of bravery and leadership were key choices that have contributed to his present-day strength of character and leadership skills.

RELATIONSHIPS

Sometimes we have an inexplicable knee-jerk reaction to someone we have just met. Our hearts might jump with joy, we might be filled with loathing, or we might have other inexplicable gut-level reactions toward this person without knowing why. In such instances, it is very likely that we have associated with them in a previous lifetime, and are simply picking up the relationship where we left off. Many people seek out a past-life regression to help them understand relationships that bewilder them.

Jessica explained to me that she was confused by an inexplicable sense of guilt and shame she felt whenever she was around her boss. He in turn sometimes became unreasonably angry with her. In certain ways, however, the two got along well, and liked one another.

> In her regression, Jessica re-lived a former incarnation as a man named Luke. Her boss appeared in that lifetime as Luke's closest friend. They roamed the countryside and had many adventures together, but Luke gambled and was deeply in debt. One night he got drunk, robbed his best friend as he slept in a rooming house, and ran away in shame, never to return.

After emerging from her regression, Jessica felt free to release the enormous burden of guilt that she had been carrying for so long—more than a century! She left the session with a much clearer understanding of her sense of shame, as well as her boss's occasional angry responses towards her.

FAYE HAD BEEN in a relationship with a man whom she had loved very deeply. After the couple broke up, she grieved to an extent that mystified her. Despite her efforts to get over the relationship, she continued to mourn its end.

At the beginning of her regression, Faye saw a woods far below her, saying it was as though she were in the sky, looking down. She zoomed in to a clearing in a forest where a small Native American tribe lived. She recognized herself as a middle-aged man, who was considered an elder, sitting around a campfire with others. This man had a son who was lying on his deathbed inside a nearby dwelling.

It had been predicted that this child would be a kind of saviour for the tribe, leading them to a higher level of being, and the child had indeed begun to fulfill the prophecy. Even though he was just a little boy, he was gifted and full of light. In flashback memories during her regression, Faye related how the father walked through the woods with his son, and how the boy's magic and laughter would make all of nature unfold. When the man was with his child, the world became an ecstatically joyous place.

Now, with his 11-year-old son on the brink of death, the father sat with a circle of men outside the tent where his son lay, and mentally and spiritually did every powerful thing he could to keep his son alive. The boy eventually died, but he would have died many days sooner had the father not held on for so long. After his death, the world became dark for the father, who lived the remainder of his life in depression and grief, mourning his lost son. The son, of course, was the man with whom Faye had had the relationship.

Because of her regression to this past life, Faye was able to understand the perplexing sense of grief she felt after breaking up with the man who had once been her son. She forgave her former self, who had not recognized that he had choices, and was finally capable of moving beyond her pain into a much happier space.

TWO MIDDLE-AGED WOMEN, Emily and Carla, had recently become very close friends and came together for a past-life regression. They were an attractive and dynamic team, and men's heads would turn when the pair walked by. Although the women were very spiritually inclined (they had met at a healing retreat), they also enjoyed going to bars, where the two of them would end up dominating the room with their gaiety and flirtatiousness. They wanted to explore the roots of their friendship.

In separate regressions, both Carla and Emily went back to recent past lives in the speakeasy days of the 1920s. While their attitudes and impressions were vastly different, the setting for both regressions was identical. Carla, the more outspoken of the two, was the Madame of a brothel, hard-bitten and edgy. Emily had come to the brothel to work under the tutelage of the Madame. In that lifetime, both of them became expert at attracting and manipulating men. (See the transcription of Emily's regression at the end of this book.)

UNFINISHED BUSINESS
ᚱ

Unfinished business is another element that may pop up when we choose to heal our present issues through past-life regression. Examples of unfinished business from our past lives might include a determination or ambition that we were unable to carry out, a love never fulfilled, or a broken promise. Such unfulfilled pockets can become persistent themes, bleeding into our present lives and demanding satisfaction.

Bobbi, a professional female race car driver, had from birth been absorbed by the thrill of speed and machinery. In a past-life regression, Bobbi discovered that she had been a young, freckle-faced German aviator in World War II with a passion for flying. His life was cut short when his airplane was shot down. The same passions for speed and adventure, together with a knack for machinery, have remained with her and persist in her present life, this time taking the form of auto racing.

BALANCE AND COMPENSATION

ℭ℟

The scales of karma demand perfect balance and compensation for what we have done in our past lives. Sometimes this can manifest in physical ways that may be very metaphorical. The torturer may be reborn with a malformed and painful body; someone who unjustly accused another may reenter life with a chronic throat condition.

Another way of balancing what has happened in our past is through our passions for particular causes. Such balances are not always negative. Jean, the Caucasian woman who had regressed to an incarnation as a black slave on a plantation, works in this lifetime as a chaplain who has an avid interest in social justice.

SERVICE TO OTHERS is another form of balance, and is thought by many to be one of the ways in which we pay our karmic dues.

James was an ardent Native American activist, whose life's work was dedicated to protecting the rights and interests of Native American people and tribes.

In his past-life regression, James found himself to be a white soldier living in North America in the 19th century. He wore boots and gloves, had a wide belt with lots of pouches, and rode a dappled white horse. The soldier looked down upon Indians as inferior and held many of the prejudices common for that time. In a skirmish, he coldly clubbed an innocent

Native American woman to death with the butt of his rifle because it was his "duty," and then rode off on his horse.

Later in that life, he felt badly and expressed remorse for what he had done. During his life review at the end of his regression, he realized that "the horse knew what I didn't." He also encountered the soul of the woman whom he had killed and tearfully asked for forgiveness from her .

SUICIDE

CR

By participating on the earth plane, we have made a contract to attend life school. This is a place of polarities and opposites, where we not only have the chance to bask in the joys of creativity and play (recess, band, art class, gym, and lunch!), but are given means to grow from life's challenges as well. Some of the best opportunities our souls have for expansion come about through dealing with obstacles and problems that are sometimes extremely harsh.

Life school is not easy. When we do not learn a lesson completely, that lesson returns in different forms until we pass the course. Some people flunk their classes and must repeat a grade! They are required to face similar experiences and conditions in lifetime after lifetime until the lesson is finally learned. A person who is unwise about handling money, for example, may face repeated instances over multiple lifetimes where finances are an issue, until she learns the lessons that her experiences have been attempting to offer her.

Sometimes, out of despair or an inability to meet the challenges before them, people commit suicide. Unfortunately, this act does not get them out of the contract. According to most beliefs about reincarnation, those who commit suicide are guaranteed to return again to incarnations where they will encounter identical or even worse conditions. Until they face their problems squarely and deal with them, they are doomed to repeat the same scenarios. There are no back doors or escape hatches. That which we have refused to face will continue to return until we grow and fulfill our soul's purpose.

Meeting our problems head-on does not mean that we will always find the ideal, harmonious solution. Life is not like a sit-com, where every issue is resolved happily in half an hour. Not all problems can be surmounted. Our lessons are not found in the results we achieve, but in the process.

Sometimes the soul's purpose is to learn such lessons as patience, humility, or courage in the face of unrelenting adversity. The good news is that once a particular test has been passed, those lessons are no longer required.

The fundamental quality we are meant to learn and practice is that of unconditional love.

GHOSTS AND HOLDING ON

 જી

Sometimes our present lives are impacted because of a person, place or event from past lifetimes that we have not been able to release.

To understand better how this works, think for a moment about a ghost. A ghost is an entity which has become stuck. Its soul has mistakenly become attached to a person, place or event, and it is miserably holding on, unable to let go, and seemingly trapped. Why does it hold on? It could be that the person, place or event may at one time have offered some form of sanctuary or love to that entity. The soul continues to cling in the mistaken belief that some day that pleasant feeling will return.

> *An example of this might be the ghost of a nun "haunting" a convent. When she was alive, she was happy in her vocation and treated well by her companions. Her spirit remains in the convent because that was where she received the greatest nurture and comfort. Attachment to that past has prevented her soul from growing and moving on as it should.*

Another "ghost-trap" occurs when entities become stuck in unpleasant situations where they reexperience over and over again the terrible emotions or traumatic events which once occurred to them, like the hackneyed Hollywood depiction of a ghost as a spirit who is trapped at the scene of his own murder. The intent of any soul is always to find loving resolution, but in the instance of ghosts, that search has been misdirected and the soul has gotten bogged down and stuck in time. Light and love, we are told, do eventually await those souls who are trapped as ghosts. They have simply gotten stuck and can't find their way out.

A man who was unjustly guillotined during the French revolution might hover in spirit at the site of his betrayal, lost for centuries in shock, and holding onto the wish to reverse his unfortunate circumstances.

What does the behavior of ghosts have to do with past-life regression? Simply this: almost all of us have a bit of the ghost within us—the patterns that continue to haunt us from our past lives! While our entire being has not become trapped in a long-past event, a certain percentage of our energy has. It is as if a fragment of our soul is still imprisoned in time, just like a ghost.

We've nearly all experienced moments of being caught up and stuck in certain emotions and circumstances, even in our present lifetime. Think of the common scenario of the rejected lover who holds for too long onto the false hope that a former love will have a change of heart—or of how some people repeatedly return to a place where they once had an enchanting experience, in the vain hope of re-creating their good times—or even of how easy it is for us to dwell repeatedly on our grief and pains. Our emotional investment in these past events is clutched tightly to our beings, often in the vain hope that some solution will occur. Such misdirected clinging can sometimes billow into a stubborn, seemingly unstoppable avalanche of resentment, unhappiness, horror, confusion, or a host of other fearful expressions that can leak from one lifetime into the next.

A portion of our soul, like a ghost, might be unconsciously replaying over and over again the past-life memory of a tender love affair in the hope that it will return, or clenching against some physical pain we suffered centuries ago, or desperately hoping for a different outcome to a serious problem from the past. That part of our soul sometimes cries out loudly. Its cries can be very bewildering. It needs resolution but does not know how to get it.

Let's go back to the earlier illustration of the nun and the man who was guillotined in the French Revolution. Imagine that these entities had not gotten stuck as ghosts and were able to move on to new bodies and lifetimes, but without resolving or integrating these key incidents from their past. The soul who had the powerful past-life experience of nurture and comfort as a nun in a convent might be born into a Jewish family, but find herself today curiously attracted to Catholicism and convents without being able to explain why. Similarly, the man who had been guillotined might have a mystifying hysterical response to anything touching his neck.

> *Troy was a skeptical man who had been brought by a friend a past-life regression group I was conducting. He didn't expect to have any experiences. After the session, he seemed unusually pensive. When we went around the group and shared stories, he revealed that he'd had a vivid remembrance of a past life where he was hung as a thief. "Now I understand why I hate neckties and tight collars so much," he said, rubbing his neck.*

A COMMON THEME among some people seeking past-life regression is an obsession with another person that defies understanding. Often they discover that they have had a past-life relationship with the object of their obsession. Recognizing the source of their feelings permits them to let go and move on in a healthy way.

> *Bill confessed that he had long been obsessed by a certain woman. He stated that for years he had strug-*

gled with dreams and feelings of love and attachment for her which defied reason, even though these feelings were unacceptable to him and interfered with his daily life. Bill and the woman had only dated briefly, and both of them were married to other people. In his past-life regression, Bill went back to a lifetime where he and the woman had been very deeply in love and spent many happy years together as husband and wife. A part of his soul had remained in that past, continually prompting him to seek the individual who had been the vessel of his earlier happiness, even though in this lifetime it was no longer useful for his or her growth for them to be together. When he fully understood the source of his obsession, he was able to let go, forgive himself and move on.

EACH PERSON IS unique. The complex and bewildering patterns that have been created in our former lifetimes manifest in many forms. One person might have an unreasonable phobia that just doesn't make sense. Another may repeatedly attract unwholesome relationships, even though she or he knows better. Yet another might suffer from an illness that has no seeming cause in present life. In every instance, it is always important to inform the present-day self, forgive, let go, and move forward with our lives. We can do this through the therapy of past-life regression.

HOW EXACTLY DO WE HEAL WITH PAST-LIFE REGRESSION?

CR

Past-life regression can uncover the hidden and dark foundations that infiltrate our being, and make sense of the cries of the soul. From the wisdom of our current lives, we have the opportunity to release those ancient situations with love, and to offer forgiveness where it is needed.

We will not heal fully until we have grown enough so that the next time we face similar circumstances, we will make a higher and more loving choice. It is not always easy to do this, which is why so many people remain stuck in their pain!

Healing comes about when we are able to face what has happened honestly, recognize what responsibility we might bear for it, learn the lessons it has to teach us, release, and forgive.

Some of the ways in which we heal include:

- *Discovering Misplaced Energy and Blocks*

- *Understanding*

- *Recognizing Unshed Tears and Clenching Against Hurts*

- *Sharing with a Witness*

- *Embracing Our Life's Lessons*

- *Forgiveness*

DISCOVERING MISPLACED ENERGY AND BLOCKS

The energy of an emotion or a thought is stronger than most people realize. Nearly all of us have experienced the feeling of receiving a "blow" in our solar plexus when another person is angry or hostile towards us. Similarly, when someone we like is attracted to us, the resultant good sensations are often very visceral. We feel "turned on," our "hearts aflame."

These are physical responses to something that is nothing more than an energy...a thought! Thoughts and emotions are indeed powerful—so powerful that when they become stuck, they can literally hurt for centuries. Many believe that memories of powerful events from our past lives are remembered and embedded in the physical structure of our cells.

Energy is by itself very pure. The nature of all energy is to move and to change. When an energy stops flowing and gets stuck and gummed up, as it does when there is an unresolved situation from a past life, it festers and begins to manifest in increasingly uncomfortable ways. The blocks that are created from such static energy are like dams in a river. They may even create weak points in our cellular tissue which are vulnerable to disease or injury.

When energy is blocked, we become uncomfortable. Such blocks are our soul's way of saying, *"Pay attention. Something needs to be released and healed here."* Usually these patterns manage to mess up our lives and our happiness so thoroughly that we have no choice but to pay attention!

Grief, pains, romances, and attachments to people, places, and things are part of the human experience. We are meant to experience them from beginning to end and ultimately to grow from them, not cling to them forever.

*We have a major task before us if we want to move for-
ward to live with the joy and love that are our birthright.
We must root out every area in our lives, past and current, where we have gotten stuck in heartache, grief, pain,
resentment, fantasy, confusion or panic—and then we
must heal and transmute those energies into positive qualities like joy, appreciation, gratitude, compassion, service,
and love. If we fail to move forward, we shall continue to
perpetuate patterns of misery, seeming victimization, ugly
relationships, poverty of pocketbook or spirit, and illness.*

In past-life therapy, our lost soul fragments or stuck energies
can be released from bondage to the past and restored to us. It is
then that healing can take place.

UNDERSTANDING: A KEY TO HEALING

When we view our past lives and find the root causes of our issues, we can experience extraordinary release and relief as a result. This can be very easy and uncomplicated. For many people, simply undergoing the process of regression and relating the story as they experience it is all it takes to heal completely.

This sets past-life regression apart from other therapies. It is phenomenally simple. By uncovering the triggering events from previous lifetimes through regression, we often receive sufficient understanding to experience closure and move on.

> *Simply by realizing that I had a past life during World War II where I was in jeopardy from airplane attacks, my fear and intense dislike of the sound of small airplanes went away. I recalled no single, specific trauma involving airplanes, nor did I expend effort in the process of letting go. Moving past my fear into comfort was a natural byproduct of understanding.*

GUILT IS A powerful emotion that can be carried from lifetime to lifetime, even though it is not always valid. If, in his past life, an individual believed that he did harm, even if he didn't actually do so, that burden may bleed into his present life and create very bewildering emotions. Two of the individuals whose regressions are included at the end of this book carried mistaken guilt.

While guilt based upon real trespasses does call for some kind of balance or karmic compensation, in the case of mistaken guilt, simply understanding what really happened through past-life regression can instantly free a person from painful emotional burdens.

RECOGNIZING UNSHED TEARS AND
CLENCHING AGAINST HURTS

Our greatest pain comes not from weeping,
but from holding back the tears!

In instances where powerful emotions from a previous lifetime such as guilt, anger, pain, hatred or shock have gotten stuck in a person's energy patterns, it is often the case that these feelings were never fully experienced. The emotions thus remained unexpressed and unreleased, lodged in the person's energy field. An individual's current life obstacles may be the result of never having fully immersed themselves in the horrifying events that happened to them. It is as if they have been walking around in a clenched position, sometimes for centuries, with their eyes closed, trying to do everything they can to avoid feeling the pain.

For complete healing in such instances, it is vital for people to remember and re-experience their past trauma on an emotional level. Tears, sighs, rage, sobs, and occasionally even screams have a great capacity to heal. Safely reliving such traumatic incidents from the past, especially with a witness present, can be the powerful cathartic needed to unplug the blocks. Notice the similarity between the words *relive* and *relieve*!

Kristal wanted a regression to explore the source of a constant, low-level and inexplicable depression she'd had all her life, even though her background and circumstances did not warrant it. She went back to a simple lifetime as a farmer several centuries ago

*whose wife died in childbirth, along with the baby. He
had not been able to express his sorrow, and lived the
remainder of his life in loneliness and choked grief. As
she relived the death of her loved ones, Kristal sobbed
the tears and felt all the emotional pain that the farmer had never let out. After her regression, she felt as
though an enormous weight had been lifted from her.*

While reliving trauma is often very healing, this does not
mean that it is appropriate or healthy to endure actual physical
suffering during a past-life regression. Rather, it is the package of
emotions surrounding the pain that needs to be faced. It would
not be necessary, for instance, for an individual to relive the full
extent of an appendicitis attack, or of a difficult childbirth, or of
horrendous physical torture in order to move on.

(While there are an increasing number of individuals conducting past-life regressions, sometimes with minimal or no training,
for this kind of therapy I strongly advise going to a certified and
experienced past-life regression therapist. Such an individual has
been trained in methods to make the session safe and effective.)

SHARING WITH A WITNESS

Reliving an event with a witness is another profound way in which we may experience healing when working with past-life regression. There is some tender aspect in human beings that finds great comfort in having another person present.

Think of the difficult experiences you have had in this life, such as an accident or the loss of a loved one. We feel terrible when we are ruminating alone about the details of our trauma, but when we share and express the identical feelings with someone else, for some reason we feel better. We also get a boost, of course, when we have the opportunity to share our love stories and successes!

A good past-life regressionist not only leads you to your past, but acts as a healing witness to the events that occurred.

EMBRACING OUR LIFE'S LESSONS

The cycle of lives and the balance of karma are not instruments of pain, although they sometimes feel that way. We have chosen to participate in human form and to incarnate in many bodies because it is an ideal way to learn the most precious lessons of the Universe. The root of all these lessons is love.

When our behavior stems from choices made out of selfishness, cruelty, prejudice, greed, self-indulgence, jealousy, lust or fear, we harm ourselves and others. Karma is an attempt to teach us another way, that of love.

A life review always follows any past-life regression that I am facilitating. In that life review, people learn from guides, from their higher selves or from their God what lessons their souls were meant to learn in the remembered lifetime. They also have the opportunity to receive a message of guidance from their former selves. The answers are nearly always clear and simple, yet vital. This can be a very healing and moving part of the regression.

Ani, the woman who had a past life in Africa where she was tricked into slavery, had in that lifetime been selfish, and neglectful of her husband and son. The message of her slave-self to the present-day woman was, "Treasure every moment you have to spend with your children." Tears flowed when Ani received this tender and very important message from her former self.

FORGIVENESS: THE DEEPEST LEVEL OF HEALING

At the core of all healing is forgiveness. In the cycle of karma, as has been stated, whatever we do to someone else will circle back at a later time, most probably in a future life, and be done to us in exact measure. This is how our souls grow and learn.

If we harm another, we must learn exactly what it feels like to be harmed in that way so that we can learn compassion and understanding. Supposing a man kills his wife in a jealous rage. It may take centuries, but eventually the soul of that man will be reborn in a form where it will experience the same circumstances, except that this time around, it will be on the receiving end, perhaps as a woman destined to be murdered by a jealous husband!

The law of karma affects us in every aspect of life. It is not limited to the huge transgressions, like physical violence to another, but includes every deed, small and large, from stealing so much as a paperclip to smiling at a grocery-store cashier. It is as if all of our thoughts and actions are riding on boomerangs, which will inevitably return to impact us.

On a note of caution: if you remember a past life in which you have greatly harmed another, be aware that nearly all of us have behaved reprehensibly at one time or another. Such a past deed does not mean that an identical injury is destined to reoccur in your present life! You may have already balanced that act in unremembered lifetimes. None of us is privy to all the extenuating circumstances of our lives, nor the precise way in which justice may be achieved.

ONE OF THE most difficult issues with which we must deal in past-life regression is the human desire for revenge. The fires of resentment keep the wheel of karma turning briskly. Even

Alcoholics Anonymous, in counseling people on how to stay sober, says, *"Resentment is the number one offender."* When we or those we love are hurt, we want to retaliate. It may take several lifetimes, but eventually we will have the opportunity—and possibly even the compulsion—to exact revenge. It is natural to have such responses when we are wronged, but it is in our best interests to overcome such limiting instincts, and instead to heal and forgive as quickly as we can. Otherwise, we are electing to become perpetrators ourselves.

Those harboring a desire for revenge or carrying a deep resentment are literally standing in line to become perpetrators in a future lifetime. It is believed that we do not always play out the scenario with the same cast of characters. Someone holding a thought of revenge in his heart may be attracted to someone else whose karmic debt or soul lessons requires that he become a victim, until the scene is fully played out.

Like an ongoing McCoy-Hatfield duel, a woman who suffered in a past life because of unkind gossip may return with an urge to talk maliciously about others behind their backs. A soldier who tortured prisoners of war in a previous lifetime might find himself a prisoner of war being victimized in this lifetime, although his torturers would not necessarily be the identical cast of characters from the past. They may simply be souls who are slated for those particular lessons.

In this vicious cycle where we dance between being a perpetrator and a victim, forgiveness is the only element that can break the pattern. When we forgive, we release ourselves from the wheel of suffering and can finally step out of the cycle.

If enough souls refuse to hurt others, eventually we will have a world of peace!

In our deepest acts of forgiveness, we actually release the other party from the need to experience the kind of suffering they imposed upon us. This does not mean that we release them to be irresponsible or unaccountable for their actions. That is the job of their soul and of their God. What our forgiveness does mean is that we are withdrawing from combat, viewing the "enemy" with complete compassion, and moving our energy to more positive, unifying emotions. It is a high order, and it is not easy.

IS IT POSSIBLE to take on someone else's karma? It may be that we contract to do this, at least to some extent, when we marry or have children. If a couple is robbed, does that mean that it was the karma of both husband and wife to be robbed, or could it be that in forming their partnership, they also agreed to participate in one another's karmic lessons? Nobody knows the answer for sure.

Healing and a release of karmic burdens are intertwined. There are Christian proponents of reincarnation who claim that when Jesus said to a man he healed, *"Go and sin no more,"* he was speaking of karma. Other philosophers have suggested that the purpose of Jesus' crucifixion was to take on the karmic suffering of any who choose to permit this, and by accepting his forgiveness for their misdeeds, Christians can hand over their karmic burdens and be reborn, as it were, with a clean slate.

SOME BELIEVE THAT once we have fully learned the lessons of compassion and forgiveness, we no longer need to be victims, or, if there is a debt to be paid, that we may instead pay our karmic debts through service. Thus, the torturer who has become truly repentant, rather than suffering physical pain,—a lesson he no longer requires,—might balance his acts by returning as a woman who dedicates her life in service as a caretaker for the less fortunate.

For those who believe that we are all one, springing from the same source, the ideal of forgiveness becomes even more urgent. It means that when we forgive others, we are essentially forgiving ourselves. When something unfortunate happens—say an individual is cut off in traffic—rather than building up a resentment against the driver who did the misdeed, one could instead ask, *"What prompted me to do that to myself?"*

In even the most grievous crimes, it is possible to move to a point of view where we can recognize that the perpetrator was simply doing the best he or she knew how to do, and to forgive that behavior. Such behavior may have involved tremendously wounding acts and poor choices...but it was still the best the other could do, given his or her background and personality.

The bottom line of all human behavior is that we want to feel good. A less evolved soul does not take into account how others may be feeling and is centered only upon making him/herself feel good.

Even for those who are highly evolved, making changes or breaking patterns of behavior is one of the most difficult challenges we face as human beings. Trying to change can snag and bruise us on many levels, which is why so many people remain stuck in their addictions and limiting behaviors. Growth is inevitable, but it is not easy. Poor choices and negative actions are often simply the result of an inability to cope and resistance to making a change, for fear it might hurt.

When we are able to recognize this—to realize, for example, that the soldier in a past life who killed our children was trying to feel good by following orders, and sincerely believed that he was vanquishing the enemy—forgiveness becomes easier.

Sometimes during a past-life regression review, the person who most needs to be forgiven is a specific individual, possibly even an enemy who may even have reappeared in lifetime after lifetime. Sometimes it is a whole group of people. Other times the person we most need to forgive turns out to be our own former selves!

Clutching our resentments and holding onto a desire for revenge is a heavy, dark burden that poisons us as much or even more than the person towards whom we feel the resentment. Those who choose the brave step of forgiveness frequently state that they feel a sense of relief, lightness, ease, and even joy. Sometimes they do not have a clear perspective of what actually occurred in the scenario until after they have stepped out of their resentment into the arena of forgiveness.

Forgiveness cannot be faked, however, nor can someone experiencing a past-life regression be forced into a forgiveness they are not yet ready to embrace. Forgiveness has nothing to do with words or lip service to the regressionist's request. Forgiveness is a matter of the heart.

This doesn't mean that we must wait until our bad feelings have gone and we feel open and wonderful towards the person who needs to be forgiven! All that is required to forgive is the complete willingness to do so. That means letting go of a desire for revenge, loosening the imprisoning bonds of resentment, opening our eyes to the truth behind the other individual's actions, and allowing our hearts to become tender.

There is no tragedy so great that it cannot be forgiven. Forgiveness pulverizes the stone walls of resentment, blame, victimization, helplessness, pitilessness and hatred that have been blocking our hearts so that love and joy can once more flow through. It is a gigantic step forward in the soul's growth and healing.

WHERE DO I GO FOR A PAST-LIFE REGRESSION?

❧

Past-life work can be intimate and profound. Tears may flow, and buried feelings may emerge. Select your past-life regression therapist with the same care you would use choosing a doctor or dentist. Ask questions, thoroughly check credentials and experience related to past-life work, find out about the other's belief system, and determine how comfortable you feel with the individual providing the regression therapy.

While you don't want to bargain-hunt for someone with whom to do this sacred, intimate work, neither should you accept overly inflated fees. If you are in financial distress, ask if there is a sliding scale, or look for a less expensive past-life workshop or group.

A personal one-to-one experience with a certified hypnotist is the preferred route for past-life regression. A group session is obviously not as personal as an individual session, but can still be quite powerful.

The better recordings and downloads offering past-life regressions still have some limitations as they are generic in their pace, the process is safeguarded so that the subconscious will not retrieve deeply traumatic material, and there is no outside witness to the process. Many people, however, find such recordings, like the Laughing Cherub CD and MP3 download *Journey to Your Deep Past* an affordable introduction to past-life regression.

A slick advertisement or web site is not a guarantee of the

quality of session you will be given. Keep in mind that someone may be expert at sales and marketing, but that does not mean that he or she is expert in past-life regression. If you feel any sort of pressure, if there are unrealistic promises, or if an individual tries to hard-sell you, run the other way fast!

WHAT IF I TRY TO HAVE A PAST-LIFE REGRESSION AND I DON'T REMEMBER ANYTHING?

ℭℜ

An experienced and expert past-life regressionist knows how to side-step potential frustration, and can guide nearly everyone to remember a former lifetime. Providing one is willing to cooperate with the steps offered by the regressionist, everybody should be capable of having a successful experience when they regress to a past life. (A failsafe method will be revealed shortly in this book.)

Once in a while, however, a person comes up against stumbling blocks during past-life regression and doesn't get anything at all. I know what this feels like, because it has happened to me! When encountering blocks, the temptation is to feel frustrated and discouraged. It is essential not to cave in to such negative responses.

What causes blocks? There are a variety of causes:

- *Sometimes blocks occur because people refuse to accept the information they are receiving as valid. They are so sure that they're making it all up that they lose their trance state and, as a result, find it difficult to proceed any further.*

- *Acute self-awareness can also interfere with the process. The more intensely an individual focuses on how the process is occurring or on analyzing the experience, the more that person interferes with the regression. The same is true if the critical or judgmental faculties are strongly engaged. When the analytical mind is in gear, the subconscious shuts down and memories stop flowing.*

• *Some people who don't seem to receive any information during a regression are simply very slow moving in their ability to regress. It takes a very long time for such people before their past-life images and perceptions bubble to the surface. If they are relaxed and comfortable in hypnosis, all they need is ample time. The many long minutes of apparent silence and blankness, however, may be misinterpreted either by them or by their hypnotist as a form of blocking—as an inability to regress. Any sense of impatience or pressure to perform on the part of the hypnotist will be picked up by the person being regressed and can easily pull them out of the trance state. An expert hypnotist is reassuring and allows individuals to take all the time they want.*

• *Having desperate or false expectations is yet another cause for blocks. Some people have very serious lifelong issues. They may have tried many different therapies without success before exploring past-life regression, and are so eager for results that they cannot relax sufficiently to access their memories.*

• *Still other people have built up enormous and unreal expectations about what their session will be like. Perhaps they anticipate relieving their problems in one profoundly dramatic regression session (which can certainly happen!), or maybe they are expecting a surrealistic, magical experience. Because of their desperation or expectations, they either become hyper-alert or try too hard and, as a result they encounter disappointment.*

I have known firsthand what it feels like to be in all of the above categories, particularly the last one. I'd seen a dramatic past-life regression on film and read many amazing stories in books, and I mistakenly thought that my past-life regressions would be just like those accounts. When nothing spectacular happened during my first regression and very little information emerged, I was disappointed.

Expectations can go the other way as well. I have encountered clients who had very diminished expectations, and who were utterly amazed at the wealth of information and healing release they received from their sessions.

In my years of practice, only a small handful of individuals have blocked so entirely that they received absolutely no impressions at all. In each case I offered these few people the easy failsafe solution (which follows!), but rather than going along willingly and following my instructions, they focused instead on their frustration, which billowed out of control and cramped the process.

I do not blame people when they have this self-defeating type of experience. The more we try not to struggle, the more we do struggle! It's like being instructed *not to think of an elephant—to think of anything in the world except an elephant.* (Are you by any chance thinking of an elephant right now?!)

Fortunately, the solution to blocking, regardless of its origin, is simple!

THE FAILSAFE SOLUTION

CR

The failsafe solution is to use your imagination. Make something up! There will be no failure if you do so. Using your imagination can provide exactly the answers you require.

During a regression, people who do not have any perception of the scene around them or who are unable to get any awareness of themselves in a previous lifetime can simply improvise. They can use their imaginations.

Remember, the information is equally valid whether it is fantasy or real, because it comes from the inner self. When obstacles that have been long held in a person's energy patterns are healed and released, the authenticity of the material triggering this healing is unimportant.

Beyond that, imagining can actually help create the scenario that will spark a real memory! A superb example of this is a woman named Gloria, who had a great fear of sharks. Gloria was positive that her fear was related to a past life; it seemed logical to her that she had at one time been killed by a shark attack. She wanted to access this information so intensely, however, and the scenario seemed so blatantly obvious, that when she was regressed, she blocked everything out and received no images or impressions at all.

Realizing that it was okay to imagine and invent, Gloria lightened up and said to herself, "All right. Sharks. Hmm. Let's pretend I'm a sailor. In fact, since I'm pretending, I might as well be a pirate!" With thorough enjoyment and even some giggles, she gave herself an eye patch, a wooden leg, a parrot on the shoulder—the whole nine yards! She began imagining herself thumping across the deck of a pirate ship. And then something interesting happened.

"Wait a minute," she said to herself. "Maybe I'm not a pirate. Maybe I'm...I'm just a frightened kid. I'm 14 years old. And maybe I'm not in a ship. I'm in a boat, like a long rowboat. And there are a bunch of drunken older guys with me, and they're rocking the boat. Stop rocking the boat! Oh, no...!" The boy was thrown out of the boat and had a fateful encounter with a shark.

This vivid and useful memory emerged because Gloria was willing to allow herself to use her imagination.

CARA HAD A troubling relationship with someone in her life that she wanted to examine through past-life regression. She was so eager to discover what her former relationship may have been with this person that she encountered blocks and couldn't access any past lifetime. It was gently suggested that Cara allow herself to imagine what kind of past life she would have had with this individual.

Cara imagined herself living in ancient Persia. The person who was problematic for her in this lifetime had been a man of great power then, and she was a much younger, intelligent woman who was his student and possibly his mistress. She adored this older man and avidly learned all he taught her. Unfortunately, someone decided to create lies about something she had done or said. When the man heard these lies, he believed them and felt that he had been betrayed.

Without ever seeing the young woman again or offering her any opportunity to defend herself, he ordered that she be walled up in a cave, where she died alone in darkness.

During her cathartic session Cara sobbed as she relived her desperation and cruel death. The lifetime she had "made up" felt very real to her indeed, revealed patterns of her current-day relationship, and helped heal. Whether the memory was true or not was inconsequential.

EXPERIMENT FOUR

Take plenty of time to do this. Have paper handy to record your impressions afterwards.

If you were to imagine a past life regarding a particular issue, pattern or relationship in your life today, what would that past life be? Now close your eyes, use all five senses and your emotions... and imagine.

THE STEPS OF A PAST-LIFE REGRESSION

ം

Each past-life regression therapist has her or his own unique style, and there is a great deal of variety in the process. Some regressionists, for instance, will refuse to do a past-life regression in the first session, but want to accustom their clients to hypnosis first. Some schedule exactly one hour per appointment and move quickly; others spend many hours for a single session.

While I often vary the way in which I offer past-life regression, depending upon the individual I'm seeing, what follows is my own basic blueprint. In the next subchapters, I share each step from beginning to end so that you can familiarize yourself with the process and have an idea of what to expect when you have your own past-life regression. It is written as though you are coming to me for an appointment:

HOW MANY SESSIONS WILL I NEED?

When you first contact me, I explain to you my preference that those who come to me for past-life exploration schedule several sessions. There are three important reasons for this:

1. *As stated earlier, accessing past lives with hypnosis is like using a muscle. Although it can develop quickly, it works better the more you exercise it. Choosing to have more than one session will allow you time to develop a sense of rapport and comfort both with me and with the process of hypnotic regression.*

2. *Most patterns have evolved over the course of many lifetimes. A single session generally doesn't provide enough time to expose completely the roots of an issue. It is much more fruitful to book several sessions than to attempt to tackle everything in one appointment.*

3. *Scheduling several appointments means that the pressure to perform and get all your answers in a single fell swoop is off.*

I ask you to book your session at a time of day or evening when you have a natural tendency to be more relaxed. Coming for your regression at 8:00 a.m. immediately after having three cups of coffee is probably not the ideal time!

PRETALK

When you arrive for your session, I help you to get comfortable. You may choose to stretch out in a cozy recliner, lie down on a couch or sit upright in a chair that feels good to you.

We start out by having a chat about your spiritual belief system and the issues that concern you. Although you have not come to your appointment for talk therapy, it is helpful on many levels for you to share with me in this way before we begin the regression. During this time, I am observing details about your personality and beliefs that will be helpful in pointing the way in which I conduct your session, and I am listening carefully to what your issues are. We are also both getting a sense of one another and establishing rapport, which is important, for we will be working as a team.

Next, I offer a little education about past-life regression, and make sure to allay any fears or misconceptions you may have about hypnosis, which is the process by which you will access your past lives, sometimes inviting you to watch a short informative video. I remind you that this session is about you, not about me. During your regression, you are completely in charge, and may go at your own pace. You have permission to move faster or slower than me, and you may always do anything you need to make yourself more comfortable...even something like getting up in the middle of the session to use the bathroom!

Telling time, sorting information, analyzing and criticizing are functions of the conscious mind. Your subconscious mind cannot do those things. As far as the subconscious is concerned, whatever it is experiencing is happening now. Emotions, beliefs, habits, long-term and past-life memory reside in the subconscious. When a person's analytical or critical mind is turned on at high volume, it acts like a screen and we are unable to tune in the subconscious.

In hypnosis it is important to turn this critical mind off, or at least have it sit out the game on the bench. You don't have to expend effort to do this; quieting the overactive mind is an aspect of hypnosis which is my job. There are ways in which you can help, however.

While we allow the conscious mind to be an observer, I suggest that you suspend critical judgment during your session and save any analysis for later. Thus, if you are recalling a past lifetime in a city where you are wearing a particular garment, you want to avoid expending the thoughts required to deduce that you are probably living in Madrid in the 1400s, as that will tend to pull you out of trance. You can figure those things out in our cooldown chat after the session.

My role in your session is simply that of expert guide and witness. I hold up the lantern and suggest the most interesting pathway for you to take. One way in which I will do this will be by asking non-leading questions, which you may choose to answer or to ignore.

When I ask you something—or example, *"What color is your hair?"*—you are to reply with the very first impression that enters your mind. For certain questions, there might be no answer; your mind might remain blank. If that happens, you are instructed to remain relaxed and avoid straining. As long as you are receiving information in other areas, it may be that the information I'm seeking is not relevant, or it may become apparent to you later. We will simply move on to another area of questioning.

Just like people on a dance floor all dance differently, everybody responds differently to this dance called past-life regression. I have had some clients begin to relive a past life literally within seconds of closing their eyes at the beginning of the session; others take an hour or more of warming up and going deeper into hypnosis before memories start to emerge. While some people follow the blueprint I offer exactly, others instinctively take off on their own track.

I suggest to you that it is simplest to follow my directions and questions, but assure you that the session is about you, not me, and I am with you for support regardless of your style of remembering.

THE HYPNOSIS BEGINS

Now we are ready to begin. I may suggest at first that you close your eyes and do an exercise, such as that described earlier in this book of remembering your bedroom. This exercise helps you to get used to the way in which your mind remembers, and to become comfortable with the sensations of focusing inward.

Next, I ask you to settle back and relax more deeply, and I assist you in entering into a hypnotic (trance) state. This is a highly pleasurable experience, which is both mentally and physically relaxing. Most people respond excellently to what is known as "progressive relaxation," in which we move up or down your body and relax each group of muscles in succession. That, however, is just one of a variety of ways to induce and deepen hypnosis.

When you are in light trance, I offer a suggestion to your deeper mind that you are free to speak and share out loud during your session. You may discover that you will be experiencing far more than you can share, so it is all right if you simply summarize what you perceive without telling me every detail. I add the suggestion that using your vocal chords and mouth will allow you to ease into an even deeper level of relaxation.

It is emphasized that your subconscious will only access material that is safe and beneficial for you to remember. This is a very powerful and important suggestion for making the session completely appropriate and safe for you, and it works.

Most people retain complete awareness of what is going on throughout the hypnotic process, just as you do when you watch a movie. In case you are one of the ten percent who go so deeply that you might spontaneously forget what has happened during your session, the suggestion is also given that you will remember everything beneficial that has occurred.

I suggest that you will be guided to the lifetime which will offer information that is going to be the most pertinent to the issues you want to work on and which will be of the greatest value to you on your present life's journey. This is a very important suggestion. It sets the intention for your session.

At this point, if it is in accordance with your spiritual beliefs, I suggest that you offer a prayer asking for guidance and protection. If I know that you believe in guides, angels or power animals, you are given the opportunity to connect to them and to ask them to accompany you on your path of exploration.

GOING BACKWARDS IN TIME

When I am certain that you are in a relaxed state of hypnosis, I will begin to take you back in time. There are many ways to do this, and each regressionist proceeds differently.

If you are a person who responds well to imagery, I might use a symbolic image to move you back through time, for the subconscious appreciates and responds to such symbols. One image I often use is that of a beautiful golden wheel with many spokes. I describe this wheel to you. Each spoke is one of your lifetimes, and at the hub of the shining wheel is God, your highest self, or your source, according to the belief system that you earlier shared with me.

You are asked to move to the spoke on the wheel that represents your present life, and to imagine yourself inside it at the point of your current age, as though you are within a comfortable and spacious tunnel or a tube, heading towards the direction of your own future. I then suggest that you turn around 180o so that you are facing your past.

If it is your first regression, you will be gently guided back in time to several happy memories from your present life. This familiarizes you with the process of remembering. Recalling only simple and pleasant moments during these "stretching exercises" is important, for it is not desirable for you to expend any emotional energy in practice.

I might say something like this: *"At the count of three, you will be back in a pleasurable, happy event which occurred when you were 17 years old. One, two, three: be there now...Take all the time you need."*

You are instructed not to force this image or to think hard about choosing a memory with your conscious mind, but rather to permit it to drift into your consciousness of its own accord.

This is relatively easy for most people to do when they are in hypnosis, and it is a helpful exercise, for you will probably access your past lives in a similar fashion.

When you indicate that you have gotten a memory, I suggest that you re-experience it fully by becoming aware of your five senses and emotions. What do you see? How do your clothes feel on your body? What sounds do you hear? What scents do you smell? Is there anything to taste? How do you feel? I ask you to share very briefly what's happening, and encourage you to use the present tense as though you are actually reliving it. It may be that your memories open like a shade suddenly drawn up from a window, giving you an immediate, clear and vivid picture of everything that is happening...or the memory may take a long time to begin forming, perhaps only in response to my questions...or you might receive just a little snippet of a scene. Each person is different and there is no black-and-white standard.

After becoming accustomed to your own unique process of remembering, I will gradually guide you backward in your present lifetime to a younger and younger age. While it is possible to have clear and distinct impressions as you float backwards through your present life, most people have only a vague and relaxing sense during this part of the regression.

Ultimately I take you back to the moments immediately following your birth. At this point you are given the opportunity to share out loud, if there be any impressions from that experience you'd like to explore. Birth memories can be very potent sources of information for some people; others don't sense much of anything, but simply drift into deeper relaxation during this time.

After pausing at your birth, I move you backwards through the time you spent in the womb. Then you leave the symbolic spoke of the wheel and travel to the point between lives where you existed just before you entered the body containing your current personality. I ask you to speak out loud and describe what your impressions are.

MOVING BETWEEN LIVES

Not everyone has the same homogenous experience, although most people agree in describing this as a place of enormous peace. Some people see colors,—often purple or blue,—bright lights, mist, or other beings. Some see a tunnel forming. Others have the impression of floating among the planets and stars. There are no rules, so whatever information you receive is exactly right for you. On occasion when I have led people to this place between lives, they have told me they are receiving instruction about the lessons they are preparing to learn in the lifetime upon which they are ready to embark.

The next step in the process is to lead you through a tunnel or hallway, such as that which people report encountering when they have near-death experiences. At the end is a bright, completely loving, all-understanding force—the hub of the wheel—which you may experience as an intense and brilliant Light. You have the opportunity for an encounter with the Light. For most people, this is a very comforting and oftentimes even ecstatic place to be. It is frequently wonderful beyond verbal description. Sometimes tears begin to flow. (The hankies are always handy!)

At this juncture, if it is comfortable and within your belief system to do so, you may request a spiritual guide or angel to join you and accompany you on your journey. Some people call upon the soul of a loved one who has previously crossed over to be with them. Others call forth a power animal.

The suggestion is now given that it is time for you to explore a past life. I again request of your deepest self that you access only those memories which will be safe and beneficial, and those which will be the most pertinent and helpful to your current life situation. You are in the hub of the wheel, and from this vantage point can easily access any lifetime.

THE ROUTE TO YOUR PAST LIVES

There are numerous effective techniques from which I may choose to assist you as you proceed to move into a previous life. Nearly all are symbolic. Some of them include:

- *Entering a hallway lined with doors;*
- *Walking on a pathway;*
- *Descending a staircase;*
- *Opening a door;*
- *Riding up or down in an elevator;*
- *Being in a garden or other landscape which is sinking or rising;*
- *Looking up at the sky;*
- *Floating down the river of life;*
- *Moving through a tunnel;*
- *Crossing a bridge;*
- *Floating on a cloud;*
- *Traveling on an emotion.*

It is emphasized that although the approach is symbolic, the lifetime in which you find yourself will be real.

My overall favorite method is to suggest that you are entering a safe, spacious, well-lit hallway lined with doors. One particular door calls to you and you will be drawn to it, as though magnetized. You are asked to stand before the door and describe it to me. The door may or may not be related to the lifetime that lies behind it. When you are ready, you are instructed to open the door and walk through...into a previous existence.

FINDING OUT WHO YOU WERE

When you step through the door, the lifetime that rests behind it sometimes unfolds immediately into a scene that is clear and vivid. Other times, however, it takes a while before you begin to ease into the memory and sense where and who you are. This is not a process that should be rushed. You are encouraged to take all the time you require and allow the story to tell itself. You may always move at your own pace.

If you do not indicate that you have begun receiving impressions, I suggest that the setting may at first be dark or dim, and that you might be only vaguely aware of yourself in form; the scene around you then gradually begins growing more and more distinct. This gives you permission to drift into your regression without pressure.

One of the simplest and most traditional ways in which you can start to receive impressions is by noticing what, if anything, is on your feet. This can be done either by looking down, by feeling what is on or under your feet, or just by an inner knowing. (I haven't yet had a client who has begun this process by smelling his feet, although it's a possibility!)

After describing your feet, you start to notice more details about your garments, and then about your physical form. As I move your awareness up your body, you will soon be able to determine whether you are male or female, and what kind of physique you have. I will never forget one deeply hypnotized woman who, when asked to scan up her body, suddenly jolted with astonishment, gestured toward her groin and with a look of absolute amazement on her face exclaimed, *"I'm a man!"*

Occasionally people are not able to figure out whether they are male or female until they have gotten much further along in the regression, especially if they are wearing some kind of garment that either sex may wear. In a few regressions I've conducted, people have at first assumed they were one sex, only to realize later that they were wrong.

After determining whether you are male or female, I may ask you to describe what color and type of hair you have, and what your hands and fingernails are like. After familiarizing yourself with your form, you are asked expand your awareness into the landscape.

I help this process by asking open-ended questions one at a time, such as: *Are you female or male? ... Is it day or night? ... Are you indoors or outdoors? ...What is the temperature like? ... Are there people around, or are you alone? ... What kinds of thoughts preoccupy you?*

We establish the lifestyle of the person you are remembering, such as your dwelling place, where you sleep and eat, with whom you live and associate, and what you do during the day.

You might launch into your memory at any point and begin a narration of your story with very little help from me. Otherwise, I will continue to ask simple questions to trigger your memories. It could happen, especially if you are experiencing past-life regression for the first time, that you feel a bit mistrustful of the information you are receiving. In such a case, you are instructed to report the *very first impression* that comes to you, even if you believe you are making it up.

Sometimes answers will arrive in response to my questions about some things, but not about others. The subconscious is very wise and tends to streamline details in a regression, proffering only that information which is pertinent and useful, and avoiding cluttering the regression with frivolous details.

Say, for example, that you have regressed to being a child in Holland walking with her father. I may ask what your father's occupation is. While I might be curious to find out, his occupation may in fact have no bearing on your story and indeed, might be a tangential distraction, in which case there is often no clear answer.

It is important when experiencing a regression to avoid struggling, which tends to bring an individual out of trance. Therefore, if you have gotten information in response to some questions, but at other questions draw a blank, it is okay for you to tell me there is no answer, trusting that this response is also an answer.

DISCOVERING WHAT HAPPENED

After your initial introduction to the person you were in another incarnation, you are guided to move to pertinent events in that existence. Generally we cover three or four key events, going to each one in turn. Some past-life regressionists move clients through their memories chronologically, even specifying the ages which they are to review, but I like to offer people the option of going forward or backward in time to any event that is pertinent.

Generally, I will word it like this: *"At the count of three, move forward or backward in time to an important event in the lifetime you are now experiencing. One...two...three. Be there now. What's going on?"*

This procedure never fails to fascinate me. A client may start out with a seemingly simple, uncomplicated memory, but gradually a story is woven, and by the time we are have covered three or four events, all the loose threads will have been knit together in the grand tapestry of a human lifetime.

DEATH

After reviewing the key events of your past life, I move you to the circumstances and events surrounding your death in that lifetime. This is done in a way that is safe, and it is important for bringing closure. No one I've worked with has ever had an experience she or he couldn't handle.

I will ask you by what means you died. Next, you share what your very last thought while you were still in your body. Finally, you investigate your experiences immediately after your soul leaves the body.

Usually people report feeling a great sense of relief and peace. Some find themselves hovering or floating above their deceased body, looking down at it, in the same way as that reported by those who have had near-death experiences. They often receive new and surprising insights from this perspective. Others relate being drawn to a tunnel or a light.

LIFE REVIEW

Your next step is to return gently to the hub, or center, of the wheel—to the Light—where you will be assisted in a loving life review. There is no judgment in this life review. You perceive the truth of the lifetime you just experienced with clarity and compassion. From such a perspective, people often have an enhanced and expanded recollection of events in the lifetime they are examining.

In this review, I ask questions, and you receive answers. (Many of the questions I ask have been inspired by the work of Henry Leo Bolduc.) You will probably experience clear and possibly surprising answers that seem to be given to you from a higher source, be it the Light, angels, guides, other spiritual figures, or God. The answers to the questions I ask you will help explain the meaning and lessons for your soul from the lifetime you have just remembered, and tie them in to what's going on in your current life. This is the most profound and healing part of the regression. Typical questions include:

- *What was your soul's purpose in that lifetime?*

- *In what way did you grow or help others to grow?*

- *In what way did you fall back or cause others to stumble?*

- *What was the happiest moment of the life you just experienced?*

- *What was the saddest moment?*

- *Is there anyone from that lifetime whom you know in your present life today?*

- *Is there anyone you need to forgive?*

- *Is there anyone who needs to forgive you?*
- *What choices did you make that currently influence you?*
- *What aspects of that life have carried over into your life today?*
- *Is there any unfinished business?*
- *What can you do to heal, integrate, or resolve any remaining issues from that past life?*

The wisdom of the answers you are given to these questions is often astonishing, brimming with revelation—and frequently accompanied by surprise. Tears may flow, and you may feel a sense of awe. Most people receive the answers to their life-review questions through an inner knowingness, as though the wise guidance counseling them is speaking inside their minds. Others hear their answers spoken, or see images. During this process, even more details of the lifetime you have just remembered may become evident.

For the deepest healing, it often happens that you are presented with an opportunity to release a situation by forgiving someone from that lifetime who harmed or hurt you. There may also be individuals who need to forgive you. Finally, you might need to communicate with and forgive your own former self.

In all these instances, you will have the opportunity to call the soul or souls in question to stand before you. Following the example of Henry Leo Bolduc, I generally suggest that you connect in at least one of three ways with these souls: *look into their eyes, hold their hands with your hands, and connect your heart to their heart.* You are free to say whatever it is that you need to say to them. They may respond by letting you know what was actually going on that motivated them to do what they did—telling their side of the story, as it were. Often this is indeed a very emotional revelation.

After this sharing, you have the opportunity to forgive them. The forgiveness process is incredibly sacred and powerful. More tears flow at this moment than at any other. It is the single most healing and cleansing aspect of a past-life regression. Forgiveness unlocks the prison gates which have been blocking our progress and damaging our souls, permitting us to release the past, with all its attendant karmic consequences, and move forward.

At the conclusion of your life review, you are given an opportunity both to give and to receive a message from your former self. This, too, is often very powerful and emotional.

WRAPPING IT UP

Before leaving your life review, I will remind you that after you emerge from hypnosis, you can easily remember anything that occurred during your session. The regression was just the beginning of a great adventure. Having opened the door to a past lifetime, you may return more readily in the future to that or another lifetime, should you wish. In your daydreams, night-dreams or meditations, further information about the incarnation you have just experienced may unfold.

At the conclusion of your life review, the steps which you took to enter into your previous existence are gently reversed. Before emerging back to normal, alert consciousness, I offer you positive suggestions for wellbeing and integration.

When you come out of hypnosis, we have a cool-down time. This is an opportunity for you to begin to assess and understand with your analytical mind the knowledge you have just received, and to tie it in with whatever your presenting issues are. I am often vividly aware of how my client's memories connect to their present-day issues or problems. Such observations are of little value unless they emerge from within the consciousness of the person who had the experience, however. Thus, although I may assist you in making these connections during your cool-down time, I do my best to avoid the temptation of connecting the dots for you. No matter how brilliant my insights might be, it is up to you to draw your own conclusions.

Generally I record past-life regression sessions, and you may take the recording home with you. You will be encouraged to record your recollections, either by journaling or drawing. It will be valuable for you to keep a record of the details of your session, and to allow time after you get home to journal and to express your feelings through art, poetry or music. Some people find that a physical activity, like yoga, dancing or even taking a walk, helps in the process of integration.

WHAT HAPPENS NEXT

In the days that follow your past-life regression, it will not be uncommon for you to experience additional insights, visions or dreams pertaining to the lifetime you just experienced. Because of these unfolding insights, it is healthy to allow a period of assimilation of a week or two between past-life sessions.

Your next past-life journey might reveal an entirely different and contrasting lifetime, or you might find yourself returning to the same incarnation to access even more information and healing.

EXPERIMENT FIVE: A FINAL EXPERIMENT

This is an experiment in exercising your mind to be spontaneous. You may be surprised by the results. After reading these instructions, close your eyes and imagine the following:

You are standing in a bedroom that has an immense closet. In fact, behind the closet doors is an enormous revolving rack holding garment bags containing every single garment ever worn by any human, male or female, who has ever lived on this planet!

Open the door of this closet. Without looking, reach in and pull out a garment bag at random from the rack. Unzip it, and carefully examine the clothing it contains. Put the garment on. Are coverings for the head, feet or hands included? Are there any other accessories? If so, put those on as well.

See the colors and visualize the details of your garment. Feel the textures of it, and how it feels on your body. Listen to the sounds it makes when you move. Smell what your clothing smells like.

Now take a few more minutes, and imagine what kind of life you lead as you wear this garment. What type of person are you? What experiences can you imaging having, wearing this garment?

TRANSCRIPTS OF INDIVIDUAL PAST-LIFE REGRESSIONS

ॐ

Following are transcriptions of three actual past-life regressions. All of them begin at the point when the individual is entering her or his past lifetime. In each case, this was the first past-life regression the individual had ever experienced. Their names, as well as certain unimportant circumstances, have been altered to protect their identities.

It is tempting for an author to include only the most melodramatic and outstanding stories as examples of past-life regression. Such tales certainly provide for the most interesting reading! While the final session fits into that category, the others I chose to include are more average examples of what past-life regression is like for most people.

I personally conducted each of these sessions. The responses of the person being regressed are in italics. Comments about the session, if any, are in brackets. Some of my instructions have been edited and shortened for ease of reading.

LINDA'S REGRESSION

Linda had a very typical past-life session. She was a well-groomed, self-possessed middle-aged woman with a pleasant and gentle manner who worked in the office of a social services group. Although her first marriage was difficult, she had been happily married for many years to her second husband, and had several grown children.

Linda had never been regressed to a past life before, but she knew self-hypnosis and practiced it regularly. She did not have any particular motive or problem causing her to seek out a past-life regression, beyond her basic curiosity.

Linda's session follows the outlines which I have described in this book. After asking that she be guided to the lifetime which would be the most useful and healing for her to explore, she found herself in a symbolic hallway lined with doors.

There is a lifetime behind every one of these doors. You are drawn to one special door. It's as if that door is magnetizing you. So go stand before that door... Please describe for me the door you're standing in front of.

It's big. It's marble. It's pink.

[The description of the doorway through which a person passes is not necessarily connected to the lifetime that lies behind it.]

When you're ready, open that door and step through to the other side...and you are now standing in form, and your form coalesces, standing with your feet firmly planted on the surface in another lifetime, another experience. Look down at your feet. What are you wearing on your feet, if anything?

Boots.

What color are the boots?

Brown.

And what are you standing on?

Cement.

Moving up your body, have an awareness of your stature and the clothing—what are you wearing on your body as you move up?

(Surprised) I think it's a uniform.

You might even feel how it feels on your body.

Picky.

And as you move up your body, you might have an awareness of whether you are male or female.

I'm a man.

Look at your hands.

They're big. They're strong. They're rough.

Go now to your head. Do you wear anything on your head?

No.

Run your fingers over your hair. What is your hair like?

It's short.

What color is it?

Blonde.

And you might even be able to see your face or have an image of what your face is like.

Strong.

How old are you—first impression?

Twenty.

Begin to look around now at the landscape around you. Are you indoors or out?

Out.

Are there buildings or nature around you?

Nature.

And are there other people around you?

No ... (with sudden dismay) I don't like this person! I don't like me!
I'm mean!

Are you smart or stupid or in between?

I'm smart.

What's your preoccupying thought?

I don't like this person!

What are you doing? Describe your setting.

I'm just walking.

What are you walking on?

(Some distress) On a field.

> [In an earlier answer, Linda said she was standing on cement.
> Sometimes people give inconsistent answers, particularly at
> the beginning of a regression. Perhaps the setting has changed,
> or perhaps the scene has simply become clearer. Some people
> even switch lives in the middle of a regression.]

And where are you going? You might have an idea.

I don't know.

All right. Now in just a moment we're going to go to three different events that happened in the lifetime of the man you are now
experiencing. At the count of three, moving either forward or

backward in time, you will be at the first key event in the lifetime you are now experiencing. One, two, three: be there now. What's going on?

I don't know. I feel better, but I don't know.

Take a moment for the scene to coalesce, and you allow all the time you need for the story to begin to form. And you have an impression of how old you are, and you do feel better. How old are you?

Fourteen?

Are you indoors or out?

I'm indoors.

Go to your dwelling place. Stand in front of your dwelling place. What does it look like?

It's a two-story house.

Are there other buildings around it, or is it alone?

I only see it.

Go to the place where you sleep at night.

Upstairs.

Describe this. You can see it, maybe even feel what it feels like to lie in your sleeping place, or maybe even notice the smells. And what's your sleeping place like?

It's a rough blanket. It's a dark room.

Is it your own room? Do others share it?

I feel like I'm alone.

What's the temperature like?

I'm okay.

Go to the place where you normally eat your meals.

It's a wooden table. It has a bench. I sit on the bench.

Are there others who eat meals with you?

I sense it, but I can't see them.

That's fine. They're not important right now if you can't see them. What is a typical meal? See it, taste it, smell it.

Bread, potatoes. (With surprise) We're poor.

You're poor. And who's "we"?

My family.

How do you spend your days?

I work.

What do you do?

I work outside in the field.

What kind of transportation do you use to get from one place to another?

I walk.

And you might even have an impression of someone calling you by name.

John.

And you might have an impression of the name of where you live.

Dublin.

Move now back to that first event, when you're 14. Something happens. Allow the story to fast-forward a little like a movie or a DVD until you come upon something that's happening. What's going on?

(Smiles tenderly) I'm with a girl! I like her.

What happens next?

We go away...

Who goes away?

The girl and I.

Where do you go?

(Excited) America!

How old are you now when you go away?

Twenty-five.

So you know her when you're 14. You might want to rewind this story a little bit, because it seems like when you were 20, you were in a uniform. What is that about?

I don't know. I don't like that.

You're very protected. Maybe you can see that part as if you're sitting in a movie theater, watching it in a movie.

I went to war. I don't like war! (Cries real tears) ...It's sad. It's so sad! (Weeping and very emotional) People die. They shouldn't have to die! ...I don't want to be here. I want to go away!

What war was it?

[While we generally use present tense during a past-life regression, this question and those subsequent to it were deliberately phrased in the past tense. Since she was distressed, this gave her the opportunity to remove herself from the intensity of direct experience, and view it instead from a safer distance.]

Potatoes. Why are we fighting over potatoes?! This is so stupid!

What happened to you in the war?

I get to leave now. I'm going away. I'm happy now.

You're happy now. But for a while you didn't like yourself, did you?

(Grunts assent)

Why didn't you like yourself?

(Crying hard) I don't want to hurt anybody!

Just look at it like you're looking at a movie—as if you're watching a movie on a screen. What did you have to do during the war?

They hurt people.

Did you hurt anybody?

I didn't want to! I didn't want to hurt him! They made me.

Did someone make you?

(Troubled) Mm-hmm.

Do you want to tell me what that was about?

It was bad. It was very bad. I didn't want to hurt him!

It was a man?

Yeah.

What did you do?

[I continued to phrase my questions in the past tense so that she could distance herself, if she chose, from the scene.]

He was going to hurt me. I had to hurt him. I had to. (Very emotional) I just had to! I'm sorry! (Nearly incoherent through her sobs)

I'm so sorry! I don't want to hurt anyone! (Sobbing even more) I don't want to kill you! I don't want to kill you!

How do you kill him?

(Through tears, still crying) I stab him.

Oh, how hard. That's hard. Let's fast forward now. What happens next? What's going on?

(Instantly shifts from grief to a smiling, bright and calm expression) We're going to America!

What's the name of your...

Mary.

Tell about what happens.

We go on a boat. ...I'm sick. (Beginning to moan and grimace in misery, clutching her stomach). Oh, I'm sick! Oh, I don't like the boat—I'm sick, oh I'm sick, oh...

(Jumping in quickly) It's okay. We're going to move right past the boat. You're better now. It's all behind you.

Okay. (Breathes with relief) I'm glad to be off the boat! Oh!

What happens next?

We find a home.

Where do you find a home? What's this new place?

New York.

Now I'm going to have you go to the second of three events, and you can fill in anything forward or backward that you want. At the count of three, be at the second important thing that happens in this life as John that you're now experiencing. One, two, three: be there now.

We're having a baby!

Where is Mary?

In bed. She just had the baby.

And where are you?

I'm by her side. I'm holding the baby. Oh, he's darling!

He? A boy?

Yes.

How do you feel?

I'm proud.

How old are you?

Thirty.

What do you do during the day?

I work in a factory.

What do you call the boy?

I don't know the name.

That's okay. It doesn't matter. Anything else happen?

I'm holding the baby. I'm proud. I feel good now!

I want you now to move forward or backward in time to the third important event in the lifetime you are now experiencing at John. At the count of three you'll be there: one, two, three. Be there now. What's going on?

(Grinning) I'm having another baby! I like this! This is a girl. Her name is Sarah!

Move forward in time. What happens next? Let the story unfold to the next event that would be interesting or pertinent for you to know.

(Somberly) A baby dies.

Which baby dies?

I don't know. I think it's a different one.

How does the baby die?

It just doesn't...never lives.

How do you feel about that?

I feel very bad. Mary feels very, very bad. We want the baby.

Fast forward to the next event that occurs. One, two, three: be there now.

I'm not sure. I'm just very relaxed. I'm very comfortable ... I feel old.

Is anyone with you?

No, I'm in the rocking chair all alone.

And you can reflect back on your life.

It was good.

Is Mary still with you?

(Softly, heartfelt) No, Mary's gone.

When did Mary go?

A couple years ago.

What happened to the children?

They're grown up. They don't come to see me very often.

How many children do you have?

Eight! (She laughs with surprise and delight.) Where did they all come from?! (Laughing)

And how do you spend your time during those years?

I work.

So now you're old and your sitting in the rocking chair. How do you spend your days?

I just look out and enjoy the view. It's pretty scenery. I like to rock and just look around at the countryside. It's very peaceful.

Where is this countryside?

I'm on a hill. I'm on a hill, like in a cabin, and I just sit on the porch and rock.

So now, if there's anything else that's important or pertinent for you to understand about the life you're now experiencing, at the count of three you'll have an awareness and you can tell and share. One, two, three: anything else about the life you're now experiencing?

It was good overall. It was good. It was a good life.

Let's move forward now. At the count of three you're going to be in the events and circumstances surrounding your death in the lifetime you're now experiencing. One, two, three. How do you die?

(She clutches her heart.)

Your heart?

My heart just quits. (Happily) I'm done! I'm done!

Where are you when you die?

(Almost giddy) I'm in my rocking chair! I'm happy!

Is anyone with you when you go?

(Contented, smiling) Nope. I'm all alone.

What's the last thought you have just before leaving your body?

I love God.

What is your first impression now after leaving the body of John?

I'm rising. I'm rising.

How does it feel to have left the body?

It feels good.

From this perspective, all the events and all the circumstances and details of the lifetime you've just experienced are even more clear and vivid. Much more information is available to you from this perspective, and you understand and see it all: all that's helpful and useful, or all that you're curious about. And go back to the Light. You're pure soul now. And you're going to have a life review. The answers are going to be given to you from a higher source, and it will all be very clear.

What was the purpose for your soul in the lifetime you just experienced as John?

Peace.

Did your soul accomplish its purpose?

Yes.

What was the absolute, happiest moment of that lifetime—the very best moment?

(Immediately) The moment I died.

What was the moment of greatest sadness or sorrow in the life-time you just experienced?

The war. That was not good.

What was your soul meant to learn in the war?

Sadness.

Were there any people from that lifetime who are people you know in your life as Linda?

Yes.

And share who that might be...

It was Randy.

> [Randy was the name of Linda's abusive first
> husband.]

And who was Randy in that lifetime?

He was the one I killed. Now I feel better about it. He came back to hurt me [in this lifetime].

Was there any way in which anything you did in that lifetime caused you to fall back, to lose ground, or to cause others in any way to fall back or lose ground?

No. I was a gentle man.

Was there anything that you did in that lifetime that advanced your soul or caused the souls of others to advance?

I helped people. I was kind. Mary was good. She was a good mother.

What aspects from the lifetime of John have continued in your present lifetime as Linda? What choices did you make or what decisions or thoughts or actions from that lifetime have continued into your life as Linda?

I don't like to hurt people. That's not good. I like to be kind. I like to be gentle. I like babies.

Is there anyone from that lifetime that you need to forgive for any reason?

I need to forgive the man that made me hurt that man.

Call him before you, the man that commanded you to hurt that man. His soul will come. Let me know when he's standing before you.

Yes.

Look into his eyes, connect your heart to his heart, take his hand in yours and tell him what you need to say.

I forgive you, Amos.

And you're fully willing to let his soul be free of that bondage and that debt to you?

Yes.

And what happens to Amos? Does he accept that forgiveness?

Yes. He tells me he's sorry, too.

And so Amos can go, when all is complete, back into the Light. You can watch him leave. Is there anyone else you need to forgive from that lifetime?

No.

Is there anyone from that lifetime who needs to forgive you?

I don't know... Does my baby, because my baby didn't live? Was it my fault?

Call the baby in front of you. Look into the baby's eyes, and connect your heart and mind. Hold the baby.

I'm sorry. (Cries) I'm sorry. I wanted you to live, too.

And you can understand what went on from this perspective, or maybe the baby, who is a soul like you, can tell you.

(With relief) It's okay! The baby didn't want to live yet! It wasn't ready. I can let it go now!

So go ahead and let that baby go ... Is there anyone else from that lifetime you may have harmed in any way from whom you now need to ask forgiveness?

I don't feel anybody.

What about the man you killed?

I told him I was sorry when I killed him. (Begins to cry again) I kept telling him, "I'm sorry, I'm sorry!" He knew I didn't want to do it.

Yes, I understand. Now, if you could give a message to the you of the past—to John—what message do you want to give to John?

You were a good man.

John has a message for you that may be helpful for you in your life today as Linda. And what messages does John have to speak to you, to offer to your heart?

Enjoy people.

Go now to the Light, to the source of all love, all understanding, all compassion, and just soak that in for a while. You did very well and you can return to the Light as often as you desire.

And it's going to be time soon for you to come back as Linda...

SUMMARY OF LINDA'S REGRESSION

☙

After her regression, Linda stated that the conflict in which she was involved wasn't an actual war, but that was the only word that came to her mind. She was baffled that there had been fighting over potatoes, and said that she was unaware of any historical facts relating to this.

History bears out her story. There were, in fact, skirmishes called Potato Riots in Ireland in the mid-1800s, including the regions surrounding Dublin. The riots occurred because the potato crop, which was the sole food for much of the population in Ireland, had failed for several years in a row, and the government cruelly refused to provide adequate relief. There were terrible famines. Huge numbers of the population died of starvation, and disease was rampant. Soldiers were sent from Dublin into the countryside to quell the riots. One report states that some of these soldiers were only given pikes, for there weren't enough guns to go around. (It is unclear from Linda's regression whether she was a soldier carrying out orders, or whether she was a rioter. Neither would have been wealthy.) The famine triggered a massive exodus of Irish, who migrated to the United States by ship. Conditions on these ships were often extremely uncomfortable.

After the regression, Linda commented that the hurtful behavior of her ex-husband now made sense. He had simply been getting even! The experience also explained and validated her innate revulsion towards war or cruelty of any kind.

EMILY'S REGRESSION

Emily was a soft-spoken and very gentle woman. Blonde and petite, she was also very pretty. There was a sense of lightness about her. She came with her good friend, Carla. The women had only known one another for a short time, but had immediately formed a deep and affectionate friendship. Both felt that they had known one another in a past life, and were eager to discover the roots of their connection.

After entering hypnosis and going to the planes between lives, Emily was brought to a doorway in a hall full of doors, each representing a past life.

Describe the door in front of you.

It's kind of a light wood. It's very tall. It has the number 4 on it.

When you step through that door, you will be in another lifetime, a lifetime that is pertinent to the life you experience today as Emily—a life that has some answers and some useful information for you. So at the count of three, step through the door. One, two, three. Stepping through the door with your feet firmly planted on the earth. You might have a sense of what is underneath your feet. And what are you standing on?

An oriental rug.

And if you look at your feet or notice what you're wearing on your feet, what if anything is on your feet?

I have black sling-back shoes.

Moving up your body, get a sense of whether you're male or female.

I'm female.

What are you wearing on your body?

It's a black dress with fringe on it.

What is your hair like?

It's curly and it's long. It's pulled back into a bun. I've got a hat on with a little netting.

What is your size or stature?

I'm very thin. I'm carrying a suitcase. I'm looking for a job.

At the count of three your name might come to you, or you might hear it later. One, two, three...what's your name?

I think it's Florence.

And what is the environment that you're in right now? Describe that for me.

It's an old home. It's like 1930 or something. It's a beautiful old home with a lot of wood, dark wood and beveled prism windows. Big crystal chandeliers. Nice furniture. Big winding staircase with a railing. It's all open ... Carla's there.

Who else, if anyone, is there?

I don't see anybody else now.

The person who is now Carla: what is she like?

She's stern. She's got some kind of kind of something on her head like a tiara or netting or something. She's got a real pretty necklace on. She's very well dressed. I can't see her dress. I just see her necklace, and it's kind of a low neckline.

What is her relationship to you?

I think she's going to hire me. I'm nervous.

Is there anything else you want to explore about this scene? You can fast forward if you like.

Yeah, let's fast forward.

You can fast forward. What's happening now?

I'm upstairs and we're drinking at a bar, and there's men there.

What's your relationship at this point?

It's a brothel.

What are you doing in the brothel?

I'm working there. I've got a lot of mixed feelings about it. I needed the work.

How old are you?

Early 20s.

How do you and the woman who is now Carla relate to each other?

She's kind of keeping her eye on me to make sure I'm doing what I'm supposed to be doing. She's not very warm and friendly.

Let's move to three pertinent events in the lifetime you are just experiencing. You can move either forward or backward in time; you can be younger or older. The first event: be there now. And what's going on?

My father's berating me.

What's happening?

He's telling me I'm worthless.

How old are you?

About 18 or something ... I'll never be anything. I didn't do well in school. I was a failure and a disappointment.

You might have a sense of where you're living.

I get the sense that it's a poor neighborhood. Really uneven sidewalks and the yards look crappy—lots of weeds. And it's dirty, dusty.

How do you feel about your father berating you?

It hurts.

Let's just move a little bit ahead in that particular event. And what happens next?

I'm walking down a street, across a bridge.

Where are you going?

Going to look for work, and I've got that suitcase. I'm not comfortable and those heels are hurting my feet. People are staring at me.

Is there more to explore, or shall we move to the next event?

Let's go.

Go to the second of the three important events in the lifetime you are now experiencing, and be there now. What's going on?

I'm stuck in that other scene in the brothel.

Let's fast forward just a little bit. What's going on in the brothel? What happens?

I met a rich man. He's very nicely dressed. He's got a black suit with pinstripes and he's got one of those watches where the chain hangs out of your pocket. He's got his hair parted down the middle and a moustache. And he's kind; he's not rough.

What happens next?

I'm nervous. He's taking off his clothes. And I don't know what to do. I'm awkward. I'm not used to this.

What happens next?

Stuck.

Move a little forward so you can just look back at what happened. Okay. What's going on?

I'm looking at a bigger home with a nice big tree in the front. I don't know whose house—I want to live there, but I don't know who's...I don't know who lives there, if it's me, or if I'm observing I just want to live there.

Well, we'll move to the next event and it will all be clear. One, two, three. Go to the next pertinent event and it's all clear. And what's happening now?

I'm having a party. I've got a big silver platter and I'm serving the guests.

About how old are you now?

Mid-30s...something.

Are you still in the brothel?

No.

How do you get out?

I don't know.

Let's go back and explore it. One, two, three: be there now. What happens?

The guy's taking me.

The rich guy?

Yeah.

What's his name?

I don't know.

[It is not uncommon for people to be unable to recollect names. Rather than struggle, I give them permission simply to say, "I don't know" to any question and move on.]

And he's taking you?

Yeah, like a Cinderella story.

And what about your relationship with the woman you now know as Carla?

I don't know. I don't think she's happy with me. I didn't stay very long there.

Let's go back now to that event where you're serving people off a platter. Be there now. What happens next?

Kind of sitting in the back yard. I'm having a cigarette. It's very pretty and peaceful, and there's big willow trees and stuff. Flowers.

And let's just check in if there's any other pertinent event in the lifetime you're now exploring to check out before we look at the way you passed. One, two, three: anything else? Be there now.

No.

So now be at the circumstances and events around your death in this lifetime you're exploring. How do you die?

I think it was cancer. I'm laying in a big bed.

How old are you when you die?

Fifties...?

And is anyone with you around the time that you are passing?

There's a woman there holding my hand.

And who is this woman? What is her relationship to you?

I don't know.

What is the very last thought that crosses your mind just before you leave your body?

I'm going home.

And now, go to the moment immediately after you have left your body. What are your impressions?

That angel is there again, that blue angel.

[Earlier in her regression, before going to her past life, Emily had an encounter with an angel like the one she now describes.]

It's time now to go to your life review, and perhaps the blue angel will be with you to help, or your other guides. And I'm going to ask questions, and the guides and the loving presence will supply the answers to the questions. What was your soul's purpose in experiencing the lifetime you have just remembered?

To rise above.

And did your soul fulfill its purpose in that lifetime?

She was never really happy. She was never really content. She had glimpses of it, but she was never really there. And that's why she had cancer. She just gave everything to everybody else. (Cries)

What was the saddest moment of that lifetime that you've just remembered? What was the saddest thing that happened?

The rejection of the father.

What was the happiest moment of the lifetime you've just experienced?

Having people around—having fun with people.

Are there any lessons or is there any wisdom from the lifetime you've just remembered that would be helpful to you in your present life as Emily?

That the circumstances aren't important; love is what's important.

Were there any people besides Carla whom you recognize as someone you know in your current life?

My father.

And who was he?

My father [in this life].

Is there anyone from that lifetime whom you need to forgive?

Yeah, him.

And are you willing to forgive him now?

(Hesitates) I want to.

That's willingness.

It's hard.

It's hard. So you may ask for help from your angel. And if you want to go ahead with this, you may call his form from that life-time before you. Perhaps you see him, or maybe you just know he's there. And let me know when he's before you.

Yes.

And you might look right into his eyes, or you might feel your heart connecting with his heart—and you're very safe. You're completely safe, completely protected. Only good can reach you—and you may also want to extend your hand and clasp his hand in yours. And what do you want to say to him?

(Sobs) I did the best I could! (Crying loudly)

What does he say to you from this perspective?

He did the best he could, too.

Do you want to forgive him now?

Yeah.

So what do you want to say to him? Connecting your heart to his..

(Breathing heavily and deeply) Oh, dad, I am so much stronger than I was before. And I've learned so much. I knew. You gave me a strong foundation in a lot of ways, but there was some stuff that you...a lot of judgment, and a lot of...he was so rigid about certain things. And my soul just wanted so to take a different path from early, early on and he didn't understand.

Talk to him.

Okay. Dad, you didn't understand. You didn't have a clue where I was or where I was going. You were stuck in your own dogma. And I know now. I just know that I'm on the right path, and I can see and put things into perspective. I can see where you were. I can see where I am. And I know that everything happened the way it was supposed to happen. And that forgiving you is a big issue, obviously, for me, and I need to do that so I can move on now and let go of all that stuff...all that baggage... leaving it there in our old house. Moving out now. I've got a new suitcase. It's full of good things. And it's full of all kind of wonderful, loving, healing things for me and for others.

Are you ready now to accept this man who was your father, this soul, unconditionally, and allow him to be who he is without demanding vengeance or revenge? Are you prepared now to forgive him fully with love?

Yes.

And so, when you are ready, with your guidance assisting you, you may tell him that you forgive him. Take your time.

Dad, I forgive you and I accept you and I love you and I release you.

How does he appear to you now?

Very sweet. He's got tears in his eyes.

Perhaps you'd like to give him a goodbye hug?

Sure.

And he can begin to fade away, and you can let me know when he's out of the picture.

Mm-hmmm. (Sighs very deeply.)

If you had anything to say to the woman that you were in that lifetime, you can go back like your own wise counselor and whisper words in her ear, and on some level her soul will hear. What do you want to share with her? What do you want her to know? You may speak to her now as though she's right in front of you.

You could have done it without that rich man. You didn't think you could, but you could've. You didn't need that guy. I'm very strong and wise, but you didn't realize it. You gave your power away. That's why you got sick. And you reached for happiness—you reached for something better, but you knew it wasn't exactly the right thing to do. It wasn't the right way to go about getting happiness, and it was inside of you the whole time. You just didn't know your own strength and your own power.

And if the woman that you were in that lifetime could come to counsel you today and offer you some valuable wisdom that you may integrate into your life that will be useful to you, what would she say to you?

She would say, "Go within. Realize that you have been given the tools, the strength, the wisdom, the talents to do everything that you need to do. It's all there. You just need to ask and allow."

The portals of memory have now been opened. More will come. You will be able to assimilate and use all this information in the most positive and beneficial way, and you will remember more about this lifetime...
   Is there anything else to look at or do before you return?

I'm just basking in the sunlight!

And you can come back many times, as often as you want, whenever you want. That's part of your soul.

SUMMARY OF
EMILY'S REGRESSION

ﾃ

There were a number of times when Emily didn't have an answer to a question, or found herself stuck. I have found that this happens most particularly when answering a question could distract an individual from the story that wants to unfold. She did not, for instance, remember her husband's name or the name of the friend at her bedside while she lay dying. These were unimportant details. When no answers came, rather than feeling frustrated, she accepted it easily and did not let it disturb her session.

While she remained fairly unemotional during the regression, her feelings came to the fore during the forgiveness, and it was powerful work. Although she initially wanted the regression simply to learn about her connection to her friend, Carla, the true lessons of that lifetime also became evident to Emily in a healing and positive way.

TODD'S REGRESSION

Warning: there is language in portions of this regression that some may find offensive.

The regression that follows is not typical. It is an unusually vivid, dramatic and emotional recall of a difficult event that occurred in a past life.

I got to know Todd a little before his past-life regression, for in the week before our session, he attended a small-group seminar I was conducting. Todd was a serious, quiet, self-disciplined man with an impassive face that rarely showed emotion. A career officer in the Navy, he had an efficient no-nonsense style.

I was impressed by his decision to trust me, and his forthrightness in sharing the issues that concerned him with both openness and honesty, despite his reserve.

Todd's primary concern was an inexplicable obsession. He was in love with a woman named Barbara, who was married to someone else. They were good friends. Although he'd sensed currents of attraction that appeared to be mutual, he had never revealed his feelings to her and often felt awkward in her presence. Todd was bewildered by the emotional depths of his love for Barbara, which had persisted for several years.

He shared with me a long list of additional issues that con-

cerned him. These included a fear of water, which had first surfaced when he was a boy; an obsession with punctuality and clocks; a fear of failure which interfered with his ability to set goals. Todd also had an extreme inability to trust. He mentioned a small incident that had happened to him a few days before his past-life regression. He had stopped at a blind intersection, and another driver had waved him on through. Although he did not trust the other driver, he went through the intersection anyway and ended up having a near miss with another car. Todd became extremely agitated as a result, and couldn't shake it off. The distress he felt lasted for hours and was out of proportion to the incident. He related that this was a typical response which inevitably came up when he was called upon to trust someone else.

Todd said that recently he had begun to have flashbacks that bewildered him. He described them as being like pictures of bubbles floating up in the water. Adding to his confusion, one morning while shaving absently he had looked into the mirror and seen another face looking back at him—the face of an older, bearded man.

[Shortly after entering hypnosis, even before I could begin my normal questioning, Todd began to groan loudly, spit and gasp for breath. His normally placid face contorted into an expression of agony, and he began to sob. A horrible moaning overtook him, interspersed with more gasping for air. Suddenly, still breathing heavily and rapidly, he screamed out in absolute anguish:]

Oh God, oh God, here we go!! Oh God, here we go! Oh God, here we go, here we go, here we go, HERE WE GO! Go on, guys. Here we go! (His sobbing and screaming increased in intensity.) Hit the beach, hit the beach, hit the beach, hit the beach goddammit. Oh my God! Oh my God! Oh my God! If you guys don't know where you are, I'll tell you, fucking A. It's D-day 1944. It's White Beach. It's White Beach.

Gonna get them fuckers! Gonna get them fuckers! Goddamn that fucking coxswain. He's fucked us up again! He gotta get us to our space on time. Fuck you! Fuck you!! Why do you think we rehearsed this so many goddamn times?! We gotta be there on time! We gotta be there on time! You gotta be there on time, because if you're not, you cannot get us to that beach...

And you did not get us to that beach, and we're too far out, and we jump into the goddamn surf...

(Todd's face softened, and in mid-sentence he made a complete and abrupt change from panicked screaming to speaking in a quiet, peaceful voice.)

...and I'm going to drown 'cause I'm too far away.... And I did.

What is the last thought you have just before leaving your body?

It's okay.

What happens right after you leave the body?

I was at the beach. And the world turned white. It just turned white... It's all right now. It's all right. (He sighs, breathing more slowly, although still heavily.)

Go in spirit now to that place of comfort, where you have a complete vision, complete understanding of that lifetime which you just experienced, and ask your guides if there's any other information that would be helpful for you to find.

Did I leave somebody behind?

And we're going to go back into it. You can go back to a pertinent event or relationship to find out more about who you were and what you were. At the count of three, you're going to go back now before the time of death. One, two, three: be there now.

It's my wife. I have to go. I have to go fight the war. And she's like: okay. And it's gone. Just for a minute she was there saying goodbye.

And if there is anything else pertinent for you to explore in this lifetime, at the count of three you'll be there. One, two, three: be there now.

(Very softly) No.

You're all done?

(Mumbles softly) Yeah, I'm done.

Okay.

I stepped off the edge of the boat and the pack was too heavy. They all died.

And if you're ready then, moving to your life review—moving to that place where you have guidance and complete answers and complete understanding.

(Beginning to breathe more loudly and suddenly very agitated; speaking more loudly) Whew!

What's going on?

Light. Really white light!

Light?

Yeah! Oh my goodness! (Smiling)

And the lifetime you just left is clear, and you understand everything, and what it meant for your soul.

Yeah. (With soft excitement and breathless) The guy I saw in the mirror! He's an older guy, but he was the fucking leader! Yeah, when I first got the image, I thought I was like a young kid, you know? Young dogface. No. I was like the sergeant, maybe. The sergeant leading the guys. And they looked at him...he was supposed to take 'em in, take 'em in, take 'em in, take 'em in, take 'em in!

[Todd, who was the sergeant, switches back and forth from describing himself in the third and first person.]

(Trembling now and weeping) And he stepped off the front of the boat and he went into oblivion. And he didn't take 'em in, and he didn't meet his mission, and he didn't keep 'em safe. He didn't do any of that!

(Choked with anger & grief) He didn't do any of it! He just stepped off the boat and went into the water, and all the bubbles come to the surface...all that imagery that's been coming all week long. He was supposed to do all of that—that was his mission! (Sobbing) That was his mission! And he didn't do it! But none of us made it. None of us made it, because the fucking sergeant went into the water and they all followed me down!

(Great anguish) And they all followed me down, and they all died on the beach. No, not on the beach. We never made it to the beach. We never made it. Oh, my gosh ... Okay. I'm okay, I'm okay, I'm okay. I'm gone.

Go to the Light.

(With pleasure and satisfaction) Yeah, it's coming. It's coming.

I'm going to ask you some questions, and the answers are going to come from the light.

Okay.

These answers are going to be important for your healing—for your completion. You don't need to let that horror and that terror, whatever was going on—that doesn't have to come up and bleed into your life any more.

(Laughs) Okay!

Your guides are going to give you the answers to these questions.

They're right here.

What was your soul's purpose in the lifetime you just experienced?

Training. Training, sir. I could train those mother fuckers.

What was your soul meant to do or learn? How was it meant to grow? Let the guides tell you or show you your soul's purpose.

Okay. That's it. "Somebody's got to be the teacher!" Wow! Oh man, this is so cool! The guides are here, and together they hold this screen, and it comes right up: "Somebody has to be the teacher!"

Did your soul fulfill its purpose?

Absolutely. These people were ready to go. They were properly trained. Poorly led, perhaps (loud laughter), but they were properly trained and ready to go.

What was the happiest moment of that lifetime?

Julie. Wedding night with Julie.

What was the time of greatest sorrow?

I'm falling into the water, and the bubbles, and grasping and stuff ...I can't see any unit. I see an eagle on my patch. I'm an eagle. But the saddest moment was to watch those cocks tumble into that water behind me. I'm watching them and they can't do anything about it, and they just...they fall behind me, and we all...I see them...that's the saddest moment.

You're going to get an image of the whole uniform, the whole rank—everything's going to come, maybe even your name.

(Brusquely) 3M. 3M. What does that mean to you, son? Johannsen! Top. They call me Top because I am the top. I'm a sergeant. Sergeant Johannsen.

You might even know where the unit came from...

I don't know. It doesn't matter, because when we get there, we're all the same. We're all part of the Army. All part of the mission.

Go back to the light now.

(Takes a noisy breath)

What's happening?

I'm back at the Light, ready for the next mission.

Are there any people from that lifetime you know today?

(Suddenly bursts into an overpowering sob) Jesus Christ! (Crying) Yeah, yeah. Yeah. It's Julie, and it's Barbara. And I...oh, man. Oh yeah, oh yeah, oh yeah. Oh yeah, mm-hmm. It's Julie. Julie was my wife. She wore pink. She wore a white collar. And I left her. I went to war, and I left Julie, and it hurt her a whole lot. And now Julie is Barbara. Barbara that I can't connect with; Barbara that I can't talk to; Barbara that I have to be so careful around; Barbara who wants to go to the past. And it's Julie, it's Barbara. Yeah, I got that.

Is there anyone from that lifetime you need to forgive...

(Interrupts) Sergeant Johannsen...

What about Sergeant Johannsen?

Joe-Joe-Joe Johannsen. JJ.

Do you need to forgive him?

No, no, no. The coxswain! [I need to forgive] the coxswain. He's doing the best he could. He's doing the best he could. He couldn't drive the damn boat. He just couldn't. But it's okay. It's okay, son. It's okay, son. It's all right, son. You did the best you could, boy. It's okay, it's okay.

So can you let him go into the light...

No.

Why no?

He survived! He had to live! He had to go back to his boat. He had to live with watching us tumble off the end of his boat, and he had to take that back with him. He'll get over it. But he's the one to forgive, absolutely.

Do you want to do that or are you willing to do that?

I just did. (With realization) Geez, okay... He represents all those people, all those drivers who want to wave me on through the intersection and I say, "No, I can't trust you."

Is there anyone who needs to forgive you?

Julie. Julie needs to forgive me for going off to war.

You can call Julie, and her soul will be present with you. What do you need to say to Julie?

"We watched too many movies together, Julie. A man's gotta do what a man's gotta do."
"Bullshit," she says.
"No, I gotta go, I gotta train these men."
"I don't want you to go," she says.
"I know, I know."
"Will you come back?" she says.
"I don't know. I don't know," I tell her. "Maybe, maybe not."

Call Julie up in the light, in this wonderful place. She's pure soul, you're pure soul, and your guides are with you now.

Yeah.

Tell her from the perspective of being in the Light that you need to tell her. Tell her anything and everything you need her soul to know.

I'm sorry I left. I'm sorry you had to do things alone. It hurts to be alone. (Sobs) I'm really sorry. (Sobbing hard) Oh gosh, oh my gosh.

Look into her eyes. Connect your heart to her heart...

Yeah.

...hold her hand in your hand.

Whew!

Does she accept you're being sorry? What does she say?

"It's okay now. It wasn't okay then, buddy. But it's okay now. It's okay now."

Her forgiveness can release you from carrying all of this. That responsibility can be gone.

Okay. Okay. Bye-bye.

And she goes into the Light?

She does. She's okay.

And you're okay.

(Jubilant) I'm here, man! I'm in the Light!

Is there anyone else you need to forgive, or who needs to forgive you? What about all those guys who jumped in after you?

*They did their job. I trained them to follow me, they followed me.
They did their job, and they're okay. They're all okay.*

Are you willing to call up JJ—Johannsen—and forgive him so he
doesn't have to carry that guilt, that burden?

[At this point in the regression it was not entirely clear to me
that JJ was the former incarnation of Todd, so I continued to
speak of him in the third person.]

*Sergeant, you trained people well, they followed you, even though
you didn't make it to the beach.*

Now hold his hand...

Sergeants don't hold hands.

...connect heart to heart...

Okay.

...eye to eye.

*Okay. Okay, Sergeant. You did your job. It wasn't your fault. The
coxswain was in at the wrong time, and you just did what you had
to do. You went over into the water, and you didn't make it, and the
guys did what they have to do. They followed you. You jumped in,
and they followed you. And you met your mission, Sergeant. You
met your mission. You don't have to apologize for that! You trained
them and they followed you. You're okay. You went to where you
need to be. You went to where you need to be, goddammit. Get over
it, son. Don't bitch, and get over it! ... Okay. Johannsen's okay with
that now.*

Let him go into the light.

Aye aye, then.

Good work.

Whew!

Your guides are going to let you know if there's anyone else from that lifetime who either needs your forgiveness or needs to forgive you.

The coxswain. I forgive you. Petty Officer Martin...Mat...what is it?

Connect your heart to his heart and look in his eyes...

Okay. Mat...Mat...Maitland? It doesn't matter. The kid driving the boat. You're okay. It's okay son. It's okay now.

Anybody else in this cast?

There was a whole lot of people in that war!

You can draw a whole group, if you need.

No. The sergeant got what he needed, the kids're okay, the coxswain, and (sighing) Julie. Julie. (Cries again)

What's coming up?

It's Julie—it's Barbara; it's Barbara—it's Julie. Barbara came into this world with a lot of pain. She had a whole lot of issues she had to deal with.

You've got your guides right there. You may ask what is the best way for you to relate to Barbara. What is the very best and highest thing you can do?

As much as I want to be with her, somebody's gotta be the teacher. Maybe later. Maybe later. But right now, I'm the teacher with Barbara. You know, Barbara's still married; Barbara needs to work through that. So right now...(silence) Right now you are given a much greater understanding of your present relationship.

Oh, yeah. That distance is appropriate. That distance is what we both need. Barbara doesn't need more complications. Barbara's got enough. Barbara needs somebody who can be detached...

You are already sensing how much of the lifetime you just experienced has bled into the life of Todd, and that can all be healed now, like a wound that's finally taken care of.

(Cries) Yeah!

And the wounds are already beginning to heal.

Why did I join the Navy? Because it was that Navy cocksucker who couldn't do his job. Those people needed to be trained better. So I came back. I've been in the Navy for 25 years so those people could be trained to do their job a little more appropriately.

Now, this is the time for you to give any last message that you want to that man you were back in the war—any message you have to give. Call his soul and speak it to him now.

He's okay.

If you were to whisper a word to him when he's in the middle of his anguish, just before he jumps, what word would you whisper that would help him?

Surface. Surface.

Now, he has a message for you, because he's been released into the light.

Same thing, buddy. Surface! Bring it out! Surface!

Go really deep. Get in that light. Soak it in and let it heal those wounds.

Whew—it's so cool!

And it's a new you, and you have a new mission. What do your guides tell you that your mission is, starting today—your new mission in life?

Find her. Find the one. And it may be Barbara. It may not be. It's okay. She'll be there. And she's waiting! She's waiting! (He laughs gleefully) Maybe you can go to the ice cream social with someone, because Julie had to go by herself. That sucked. That wasn't fun. The widow Johannsen. Poor woman. Her husband was a war hero. But how did that help her at night? Not very damn much. Poor Julie...but she's okay. She told me it was okay. She came back, and she came into another life.

Surface, Buddy, surface. (Muffled and very soft, emerging a little from the hypnosis) Do you know how much this clears up? Do you have any idea how much this clears up? Oh, man, all the water that I couldn't go into as a boy! You know where we went? I was just a boy; I was just a little kid and they took me to the beach. "No, don't put me in that water. Do not put me in that water." You know where it was at? Omaha, Nebraska! Where was that lifetime? Omaha Beach! Somebody figure this out!

Would somebody figure this out?! Yeah, Omaha Beach—Omaha, Nebraska. Do you know how much this clears up?

Let's ask your guides if there's anything else that you need to visit for your healing and your release.

Yeah. Here's the list: Water—Taken care of. Time—The coxswain's gotta be there on time. The coxswain has got to be there on time. The tide has got to be right. That clock. You've got to pay attention to that clock. Trust—And you don't trust the boys who can't drive the boat. Maybe you should learn to trust just a little more.

Check down the list. Anything else?

Water. Time. Trust. Goals... You've got to make goals. I don't want to make goals, because perfection is the only acceptable standard. The only way to be perfect is to not fail, and the only way you will not fail is if you do not try, and if you do not try, you will not fail, so we will not set goals. (Slow whisper) And if we do not set goals, we just never get there...

What do your guides have to tell you about failure?

Aim high. Have perfection as a goal, as a target, but not as the only acceptable standard. Oh, yeah. You want to have high standards, but you want to actually have them such that you can actually work toward them. It's okay to set goals. Oh. Oh. Yeah, okay...And the other one that's on the list: tenacity. Tenacity...you just walk away when it gets kind of tough, don't you boy? You just kind of walk away.

Who's saying that to you?

I'm not sure. I think it's the sergeant.

What do your guides say?

Listen. Don't get wound up. Just use it. Build that bridge, get over it, it's okay. Tenacity doesn't all have to come tomorrow. You don't hang onto the bull and ride it into the dirt. You just let go when you need to let go, but you hang on as long as you can hang on. You get your full eight seconds, you win a prize; you don't get your full eight seconds, everybody at the rodeo still claps for you. They're glad you rode the bull for as long as you could.

What else is on the list?

Let's review for a moment, shall we? Water. Time. Tenacity. Goals. Failure. Clock. Trust. I think that pretty much covers it.

And Julie/Barbara.

Oh, yeah. Oh, yeah. That's gonna be hard, but I'm gonna do it somehow. I'm gonna get some guidance before I go back and face Barbara. It's okay.

Anything else in the light? Anything else for completion, healing, feeling good?

No. Whew! No.

SUMMARY OF
TODD'S REGRESSION

ᘓ

While I caution people not to expect one past-life regression to address all of their life's issues, it certainly can happen, as it did in Todd's case. His lifetime as Joe Johannsen, the sergeant in World War II who left his wife to go to war, trained his men, and finally jumped off the boat too early, drowning in the deep water with his men following him to their deaths, offered him the understanding he needed for all of his perplexing issues.

Research done on D-Day landings at Omaha Beach verifies Todd's story. There was a section of the beach called White Beach. The gear and packs the men who jumped into the water carried on their backs were so heavy that they sometimes toppled even when they landed in shallow water. In deep water, they would have no chance of survival. Unfortunately, there were a number of instances where frightened or misguided coxswains made mistakes, thinking they had come aground when in fact they were still in deep water.

At the end of his session, Todd told me he suddenly realized why he had chosen to become a career officer in the Navy.

Grinning, he said, "This time, I came back to get it right!"

CONCLUSION

Our connections with our past selves are powerful beyond description. Through the process of past-life regression, we have the extraordinary opportunity to integrate, mend, soothe and eliminate toxic parts of ourselves that may have been stuck, dormant or lost for centuries. We may also renew long-buried gifts, and recognize our intrinsic goodness. Deep understanding and healing result when we open the door for loving exchanges with our former selves through past-life regression.

"Your hearts know in silence the secrets of the days and the nights. But your ears thirst for the sound of your heart's knowledge. You would know in words that which you have always known in thought. You would touch with your fingers the naked body of your dreams. And it is well you should."

Kahlil Gibran
from "The Prophet"

ABOUT THE AUTHOR

MARY ELIZABETH RAINES has trained people from all over the world to become past-life regression counselors. The founder of the Academy for Professional Hypnosis Training, she has been featured in articles about past-life regression, and has been a guest on radio and television shows.

According to the National Guild of Hypnotists, where she has been an adjunct faculty member since 2000, Raines is *"recognized as one of the leading practitioners of the art and science of hypnotism."*

She has given workshops and talks on past-life regression throughout the United States, and is the author and narrator of the Laughing Cherub CD and MP3 series, which includes *Journey to Your Deep Past*, a recording that allows listeners an opportunity to experience their own past-life regression.

A published writer since the 1970s, she has won several prizes for her writing, contributed chapters to three books on hypnosis, worked as a newspaper reporter, and been a columnist for *The Journal of Hypnotism*. In addition to her nonfiction, Mary Elizabeth Raines is a playwright and the author of a novel, *UNA*.